AWAKENING

THE

SLEEPING

GIANT

Church Re-Discovered

John C. Hoogeveen III

Published by Made The Exchange Media Lab, Michigan.
©2021 by Made The Exchange Media Lab, LLC.

ISBN 978-1-7379879-0-1 (pbk)
ISBN 978-1-7379879-3-2 (hardcover)
ISBN 978-1-7379879-1-8 (pbk)

Scripture quotations are taken from the
New International Version/ The Message Parallel Study Bible,
Zondervan Publishing, Copyright ©2008 and Bible Hub,
www.biblehub.com

Made The Exchange Media Lab
Michigan

AWAKENING

THE

SLEEPING

GIANT

Church Re-Discovered

Contents

Dedicated to the church

Preface

This book is compiled of research, personal experience, and biblical study of the church Jesus Christ founded in the New Testament. I knew, at least to some degree, I was embarking on a daring journey likely to leave many leaders holding onto traditions modeled by the North American Church structure unsettled. I could not, however, turn away from what I believed the Lord was asking me to do. Eleanor Roosevelt once said, "Do one thing every day that scares you." Well, this book results from hundreds of days that have scared me. I have been scared for two reasons. The first is selfish because I know the following content will not make me popular, and secondly, I know what could happen if the church is not *re-discovered*. It is the second that drives me, developed out of love for God, His church, and you.

There is no doubt that the North American Church has had a significant impact on the world. Thousands of lost individuals come to know Jesus as their Lord and Savior every week, and the name of Jesus can be heard around the world because of how God has used the North American Church. For that, we praise God. However, what God uses for his glory cannot be used to justify the actions thereof. God does what God does; He will use all things, good, bad, or indifferent, to bring Him glory.

I realized that the church modeled for us by Jesus is not being reflected in most churches in North America. I was not sure what was missing, or if anything was missing; I just knew that I had to figure out what God's design of and desire for the church is, to make sure that I was teaching on and building a faithful church Jesus would be pleased to claim.

It all started with inner conflict, as many projects do. I was torn between two ideas of the church being presented to me by two influential people in my life; one was a pastor and the other a former pastor turned missionary. The problem was not that one seemed right, and the other seemed wrong; in fact, both ideas made sense. They were, however, far from being the same. Thus, the inner conflict began, and the Lord asked me to find out for myself through the leading and teaching of the Holy Spirit.

On an airplane headed to San Juan, Puerto Rico, from Philadelphia, Pennsylvania, the Lord spoke and asked me to write down what I believed the *Bible* teaches about the church. What I discovered on this journey was challenging to accept and even more challenging to apply. It has become increasingly more difficult to share with those who only know what tradition has taught them. I have received mixed feedback as I discussed my research and study results with others. It ranged from positive and affirming encouragement to rejection and what some may consider persecution. On a personal level, persecution came in the form of getting fired from a pastoral position after expressing and living out the biblical model of church, which this book will lay out. However, instead of affirmation, rejection, and persecution, the Lord has given me the grace to see and a vision for how to restore His church.

Introduction

The Church (*Ecclēsia*) Defined

Ecclēsia according to the Strong's Concordance:
"People called out from the world and to God, the
outcome being the Church (the mystical body of Christ) –
i.e., the universal (total) body of believers whom God calls
out from the world and into His eternal kingdom."
The church, as described in the bible, is the Ecclesia. It is
the only word used for church, the universal church,
meaning all believers and the gathering as a local church.

People are creatures of habit. Although behaviors like brushing your teeth or taking a shower each day are considered good habits in most cultures, there are also practices that are not good for you. In Matthew 28:16-20, Jesus gives his disciples their final command, *"Go therefore and make disciples of all nation, baptizing them in the name of the Father, and of the Son, and of the Holy Spirit, teaching them to obey all the things I have taught you...."* The fulfillment of Jesus' command should be the result of what the church practices. The premise of this book is to discuss the different practices found between the *New Testament Church* modeled for us in the Bible and what we see in the *North American Church*—in the end, offering biblically-based practices that can help re-direct churches in North America to better reflect the biblical model of church.

At the beginning of each chapter, the reader will have the opportunity to assess where they are currently by answering a few simple questions. Questions are also provided at the end of each chapter that may be helpful for thinking through what the reader's next steps might look like.

Although some change in church practice is inevitable, and modifications may be argued based on cultural differences and technological advancement (which has led to numerical church growth), a question must be asked. How much can something change before it becomes something different altogether?

Let me share an example with you. I enjoy cars and have since I was a child. In my opinion, the 1985 Porsche 959 is the cream of the crop. Classic American Muscle Cars, however, are some of the most sought-after vehicles today. Owning a 1979 Chevy Camaro myself, with a 350 Corvette engine with a top speed of at least 160 mph (don't ask me how I know this) as my first car helps make my point. There is something about solid steel, big-block engines, a four-barrel carburetor, and a rumble that makes you quiver that cannot be explained. One such car is the Dodge Charger. Originally the Dodge Charger was a two-door sports car. Now it is marketed as a four-door sedan (albeit a successful marketing plan). But as Christian Seabaugh with *MotorTrend Magazine*[1] notes, "When Dodge re-launched the

Charger[2] nameplate in 2006, it got some flak from traditionalists for what it wasn't: a two-door muscle car like the iconic Dodge Chargers of the late '60s. Instead, it was a front-engine, rear-drive sedan with an optional V-8 in an era of boring beige boxes." Although Dodge utilized a classic name many people knew, diehards were not impressed. Is the modern vehicle that Dodge calls the Charger really a Charger? I am no car expert, so I will let you make your own decision here. But I think you get my point. People tend to stick familiar labels on things that are not what the original label was. This is precisely what has happened with the church in North America. In this book, the North American Church will be looked at from the same angle, asking a similar question, "Is the organization that North Americans call church really the church?"

Many stumbling blocks often blind the church to what Jesus intended her to be. Emotions tied to traditions are usually the main contributing factor in changing them. Although our emotions can make things seem very real, Mark Batterson, in his book *Draw the Circle,* says that the emotions people experience do not reflect their external reality but rather they

---

[1] MotorTrend Magazine. (2021). MOTOR TREND GROUP. https://www.motortrend.com/

[2] Dodge. (2021). FCS US. https://www.dodge.com/charger.html

reflect their internal reality. In other words, our emotions tied to church tradition cannot justify the tradition because the emotions tied to them cause us to see and understand the church as we are, not as the church is. Unfortunately, emotions have led the church in North America down the road it is on today, having hierarchy systems and being consumer-minded rather than producer-minded. A mantra for the North American Church has been, *come and hear*, rather than *go and share*.

How do we work past our emotions to see reality as it really is? One might say that we must approach the church through a spiritual lens rather than a worldly one. This is only possible by going beyond our limits as human beings, past rational and logical thinking, and past our senses to a place only the Holy Spirit can take us. The Holy Spirit can move us from an emotional response to a spiritual response, and this is accomplished through humbly going to the Father in prayer, fasting, and the study of Scripture. My hope is that the church is provided tangible information and tools to begin applying and sharing the New Testament principles so that the church can once again change the world.

A Word of Caution

This book is meant to be a sort of relational conversation between the author and the reader, but I wish to offer you a word of caution before you read on. My goal is not to defame, discount, or discredit the North American Church or those who lead it. Instead, it is to reveal how the church Jesus modeled for us can be restored and how we as followers can fulfill the Great Commission by applying and sharing what He taught. For those not prepared to be challenged and changed, this book may not be for you.

For Those Who Choose to Continue Reading

In the end, through the Holy Spirit's leading, you will need to decide for yourself what changes are made. Please commit to reading this book to completion to fully grasp what the Lord has laid on my heart to share with you. Please give me grace as you read through these pages, as this was as hard to write as it will be to read. The Lord has challenged me to re-evaluate my idea and definition of the church through this process. Also, please do your homework. Do not take *my word* for it, instead discover God's intended design and desire for *His church* yourself by digging into *His Word*. Welcome to the journey. Let's begin awakening the sleeping giant.

I leave you with one last note, given to us by the Apostle Paul, before you read on:

By the grace God has given me, I laid a foundation as an expert builder, and someone else is building on it. But each one should be careful how he builds. For no one can lay any foundation other than the one already laid, which is Jesus Christ. If any man builds on this foundation using gold, silver, costly stones, wood, hay, or straw, his work will be shown for what it is, because the Day will bring it to light.
It will be revealed with fire, and the fire will test the quality of each man's work. If what he has built survives, he will be rewarded. If it is burned up, he will suffer loss; he himself will be saved, but only as one escaping through the flames.
- 1 Corinthians 3:10-15

Chapter 1

Pre-Chapter Assessment Questions

1. How would you describe the structure of the church you currently attend?

2. What influences does your church consider when making decisions (social, local, national, in-house, out of house, etc.)?

3. Would you consider your current church leadership to be set up like a hierarchy or plurality of elders/priesthood of all believers?

4. Would you consider your current church structure to be consumer-minded (come/invite others to hear) or producer-minded (go/equip others to share)?

Outside Influences

How the local church lives out and effectively brings Gospel-centered change to a community depends greatly on how it is structured. If we took the time to look at most churches in North America, we would find that the organizational structure seen in the modern North American Church (NAC) is a centralized model rather than a decentralized model. This simply means that what the/a church does, believes, and teaches revolves around an institution, denomination, or organization. Francis Chan shares some insight as to why this might be, with this thought-provoking statement, "God gave us his "order" for the church. He told us precisely what He wanted through His commandments in the Bible. In our arrogance, we created something we think works better." Ouch. But can we honestly deny it? Can we deny that many outside sources, which do not necessarily have the Gospel in mind, have influenced how North American Christians "do church"? These "things" that Chan is referring to can include businesses, government, social media, television, radio, other media outlets, secular non-profits, Christian non-profits, income, status, family and/or friends and are all areas that have influenced many church leaders lending to the implementation of many structural elements seen in churches today.

3

Could it be that the resulting structural elements defining so many churches, such as budgets, programs, location, worship style, aesthetically pleasing buildings, staff members, entertainment, and 501(c)(3) non-profit registration, among others, are results from outside influences rather than biblical ones? It would seem that the above structural elements complicate what was designed to be simple. I feel it is essential for me to note I am not necessarily saying these structural elements are intrinsically bad in and of themselves. However, when used for church growth and multiplication, they typically end up being the main focal point rather than Jesus. Meaning what a church does structurally is how the church will attract people to church services, not Jesus and the message he brings. Jesus ends up being the result of participation, not participation being the result of Jesus. The ramifications of this are more significant than one might think. The emphasis, then, is put on mankind, their desires, abilities, and/or limitations rather than focusing on the desires, will, and unlimited ability of God. Clearly, this is not God's intention. Thus, the church has become a human-designed, run, led, and maintained organization while minimally relying on God's Word to model it after, putting Jesus second to mankind.

Before we move on, please understand that I am not calling out church leaders or individuals, and this has nothing to do with *Spirit-led* desires, hopes, goals, or motives. The issues lie within the current structural elements of the church themselves, which leads to compromise. *The structure demands the outcome.* No matter how passionate and/or genuine leaders are, no matter how strong their faith is or how much they love Jesus, the current structure found in most North American churches will ultimately lead to the compromise of biblical truth and the results thereof. There is no other alternative under the current model. I reiterate this point several times throughout this book as I long for you to understand that the issue is the existing structure, not necessarily the people implementing it. Again, *the structure demands the outcome.* Maybe an example will help.

I enjoy cooking, especially grilling. There are some structural elements used when I grill. The meat, grill, fuel, and food thermometer are all structural elements of grilling. I can, without a doubt, tell you the result of a beefsteak grilled on my gas grill, cooked to 145 degrees. It will be browned on the outside, the fat will be slightly crispy yet not too crispy where it's hard, and the meat will be medium-rare. Why can I tell you this? Because the structure of the process demands the outcome. There is no other option. The meat will not be rare, and it will not be well-done. No matter how much someone may want their steak well done, no matter how good or bad of a grill master you may be, if using the above structural elements/parameters there is only one possible outcome, a perfectly cooked beefsteak that melts in your mouth (of course this is only my opinion), there is no other outcome. The structure demands the outcome. Change the structure, change the outcome.

Ideas influenced by the outside, i.e., the world, are so invasive that numerous extra-church or para-church companies and ministries have been developed and launched focusing on helping churches with their structural elements. An important note, these companies, or ministries I am referring to do not consider themselves to be part of the local churches which they take on as clients, but rather are separate entities outside of these local churches. Although they may attend, or be members of a church, their focus is not "their" church per se, in fact, their gifts might not even be utilized by the church they attend; they are service providers providing services to clients.

One such company focuses on helping churches get their individual 501(c)(3) non-profit status. Their website reads,

> It has never been easier to get started! The Get Started Plan (name changed) has helped thousands of churches obtain 501(c)(3) tax-exempt status and establish a strong foundation

that protects what God has given them to lead. This proven system results in maximized protection while building strength on which to grow.

Although this company may help many churches obtain their non-profit status, the underlying message is that a strong church foundation relies on: (1) it's non-profit status (2) strength comes from its financial state (3) protection that comes through this organization. Meaning, that when their methods and practices are implemented, your church will be protected. Intrinsically, there isn't necessarily anything wrong with churches holding a 501(c)(3) status. However, the main source of protection for churches must not be their non-profit standing. A 501(c)(3) can be used as a supporting role, if used at all, but mustn't be seen as necessary. The issue is deeper than a church's non-profit status though. When Jesus told the rich young ruler to go sell everything and follow him, *Jesus was not saying having money was bad, he was testing the rich man's heart.* Of course, we may never know for sure, but it may be said that if the rich young ruler was willing, Jesus might have told him to keep it, like what he did with Abraham in the case of sacrificing his son Isaac. Jesus is not concerned with 501(c)(3)'s or any other structural element for that matter, he is concerned with our heart. Jesus wants to know if we are willing to leave it all behind to follow him, if/when the time comes to do so. Sadly, many churches and people do with these structural elements what the rich young ruler did with his wealth.

In contrast to the aforementioned stance concerning 501(c)(3)'s, the Bible teaches us that a strong foundation, strength, and protection is found in Jesus:

"For who is God besides the Lord?
And who is the Rock except our God?"
- Psalm 18:31

"But the Lord has become my fortress,
and my God the rock in whom I take refuge."
- Psalm 94:22

"For no one can lay any foundation other
than the one already laid, which is Jesus Christ."
- 1 Corinthians 3:11

"...built on the foundation of the
apostles and prophets, with Christ Jesus himself as
the chief cornerstone." - Ephesians 2:20

"Nevertheless, God's foundation stands firm,
sealed with this inscription..." - 2 Timothy 2:19

"The Lord is my light and my salvation whom shall I
fear? The Lord is the stronghold of my life of whom
shall I be afraid?" - Psalm 27:1

"The Lord gives strength to his people..."
- Psalm 29:11

"He gives strength to the weary and increases the
power of the weak. Even youths grow weary, and

8

*young men will stumble and fall but those who hope
in the Lord will renew their strength."*
- Isaiah 40:29-31
*"Finally, be strong in the Lord and
in his mighty power."* - Ephesians 6:10

*"For God did not give us a spirit of
timidness, but a spirit of power,
of love and of self-disciple."* - 2 Timothy 1:7

*"I can do everything through him
who gives me strength."* - Philippians 4:13

*"Be strong and courageous. Do not be afraid or
terrified because of them, for the Lord your God
goes with you; he will never leave you nor forsake
you."*
- Deuteronomy 31:6

*"So do not fear, for I am with you; do not be
dismayed, for I am your God. I will strengthen you
and help you; I will uphold you with my righteous
right hand."* -Isaiah 41:10

*"But the Lord is faithful, and he will strengthen and
protect you from the evil one."* - 2 Thessalonians 3:3

The truth provided by the Lord, just in these verses alone,
provides enough evidence to realize that the above
company/ministry does not align with God's intention found
in the Bible concerning where a church's strength and
protection come from.

9

Another ministry offers guidelines for church structure. Some of these structural guidelines are church planting assessment, project management, fundraising, and management teams. Again, we are not saying here that these guidelines are wrong in and of themselves; we are simply looking at and comparing them to what the Bible teaches concerning church growth, development, and structure.

With that being said, Acts 2:42-47 presents the *timeless* model given to us by God to mirror:

> *They devoted themselves to the apostles' teaching and to fellowship, to the breaking of bread and to prayer. Everyone was filled with awe at the many wonders and signs performed by the apostles. All the believers were together and had everything in common. They sold property and possessions to give to anyone who had need. Every day they continued to meet together in the temple courts. They broke bread in their homes and ate together with glad and sincere hearts, praising God and enjoying the favor of all the people. And the Lord added to their number daily those who were being saved.* - Acts 2:42-47

I hope that any pre-existing fog is beginning to fade away and that clarity is developing. Rather than being *devoted to one another in Christian community*, the NAC has become a complicated business structure involving separate companies/ministries, many providing methods solely focused on helping a church get its start. As noted previously, these are not necessarily bad but are not the methods found in the

Word of God, which is sharing the gospel, baptizing believers, gathering as a Christian community, being obedient to Christ's commands, and growing in numbers because God adds to them.

How a large majority of Christians relate to those living near them offers more evidence of the church's shortcomings in being devoted to one another in Christian community. The authors of *The Art of Neighboring* highlight that many Christians do not know much more about their neighbors than their names, and many do not even know that. I must admit, I am just as guilty of this as anyone else, but the fact remains, the Bible teaches the church to:

"...love your neighbor as yourself."
- Matthew 19:19

"... 'Love your neighbor as yourself.'
There is no commandment
greater than these." - Mark 12:31

"For the entire law is fulfilled in keeping this one
command: "Love your neighbor as yourself." If you
bite and devour each other, watch out or you will be
destroyed by each other." - Galatians 5:14

"Teacher, which is the greatest commandment in the
Law?" Jesus replied: "'Love the Lord your God with
all your heart and with all your soul and with all
your mind.' This is the first and greatest
commandment. And the second is like it: 'Love your
neighbor as yourself.' All the Law and the Prophets

11

hang on these two commandments." - Matthew 22:36-40

"Let no debt remain outstanding, except the continuing debt to love one another, for whoever loves others has fulfilled the law. The commandments, "You shall not commit adultery," "You shall not murder," "You shall not steal," "You shall not covet," and whatever other command there may be, are summed up in this one command: "Love your neighbor as yourself." Love does no harm to a neighbor. Therefore, love is the fulfillment of the law." - Romans 13:8-10

If you believe that you are as guilty as I am of these shortcomings, the remedy is to continually pray in the Spirit, and engage with God's Word, asking the Lord to reveal any error and to give direction as to how to follow His plan more faithfully. I want to encourage you with what the Lord teaches us through James 1:2-8:

Consider it pure joy, my brothers and sisters, whenever you face trials of many kinds, because you know that the testing of your faith produces perseverance.
Let perseverance finish its work so that you may be mature and complete, not lacking anything. If any of you lacks wisdom, you should ask God, who gives generously to all without finding fault, and it will be given to you. But when you ask, you must believe and not doubt, because the one who doubts is like a wave of the sea, blown and tossed by the wind. That person should not expect to receive anything from the Lord.

Such a person is double-minded and unstable in all they do.

When the Lord opened my eyes to the reality of this Scripture it felt like a double-edged sword piercing my heart. But I want to encourage you that although the pain of understanding our own weaknesses can sometimes seem unbearable, God's love and power overcome our pain every time. To quote a good friend, "God never asks his faithful to do anything easy. The heroes of faith were asked to do difficult things."

Being that we are talking about the church in North America, we could say that the genesis of its structure rests on capitalism. This capitalist beginning leads to ulterior motives that subtly develop over time that reinforces structure and policy over flexibility for the Spirit to lead. Although capitalism may be considered a fantastic model for entrepreneurship and making money, *the church was never meant to be a capitalist endeavor.* As we will see, one of the major structural elements of the NAC forces it into a business church model rather than a biblical church model.

Butts in Seats

Many of us are walking around with an unknown agenda when making friends and/or inviting people to a church service. It has been suggested that many Christians befriend non-believers simply to lead them to faith. Are we guilty of this? Looking at how church leaders promote invitation, I think we can agree we are. Too often Christians only attempt to connect with those they do not know when there is a specific push from their local church to invite others. This leads to questions about the role of a church; Is it to allow the Spirit to do a work among believers so they are empowered to go and make disciples of all nations (Matthew 28:16-20), or to become friends with people to get them to church? The existence of these questions highlights the constant battle between numbers (founded on structure) and genuine relationships (founded on love). This battle seldom, if ever, results in a true Christian community because people can often see the hidden agenda, which can cause more harm than good.

Not unlike a business owner with an agenda driven by how many people buy their products and/or services, most church leaders have agendas driven by how many people attend their church and give regularly. As a result, their church structure will be built to serve that agenda. While businesses have an obvious and intentional agenda revolving around attracting customers or clients, many churches have an unintentional hidden, yet necessary, agenda revolving around attracting attendees who give and invite others. The business/ministry

14

structures result in these agendas naturally developing out of needs created by the structures themselves and therefore are unavoidable. Both agendas exist to meet the same need, and that need is based upon incoming finances. A particular agenda often set for churches is what can be called the *"butts in seats agenda."*

When discussing his job description, Larry (name changed), senior pastor of a 5000-member church, asked me, "Do you want to know what my job description was as a senior pastor? To get butts in the seats and get them to give as much as they can." Larry is not the only pastor that shares this same goal. This job description and resulting *"butts in seats agenda"* is evidence that getting people to attend church and give financially is the driving force behind what a local church does.

In researching the economics of churches, Bird found that those who attend church services on a regular basis tend to give a higher percentage of their income to charity, including their church. Thus, the resulting *"butts in seats agenda".* Although not intentional, this agenda is transferred to the body and affects how and why a church does certain things and not others. Almost everything the local church does revolves around getting people in the doors, getting them to stay, and getting them to give financially. Ironically, the Bible teaches that the love of money is the root of all sorts of evil;

"For the love of money is a root of all kinds of evil. Some people, eager for money, have wandered from the faith and pierced themselves with many griefs." (1 Timothy 6:10).

Who's The Boss

More than just the outside influences leading to the physical structural elements and a *"butts in seats agenda"*, leadership in the NAC also reflects much more of the business model than the church seen in the New Testament. Many churches operate under a staffed hierarchy structure with the senior pastor on the top, like a CEO. Similar to the corporate ladder, the senior pastor is often seen as "extra holy" or "special" because of his position. An unfortunate result is that the power of position downplays the gifts Jesus gave to the church that Paul wrote about in Ephesians 4:11. This often results in a boss-employee relationship among pastors and church leaders/staff. Misrepresenting what the Bible calls the *priesthood of all believers* (1 Peter: 2-5). In some ways this is like the scene in the miniseries, *Band of Brothers*[3]; a soldier disrespects his commanding officer due to a disagreement and is told, "We salute the rank, not the man." A sort of, what the pastor says goes mentality develops. Because of this

---

[3] Band of brothers, (2001), HBO Home Entertainment.

expectation of respect and power, churchgoers often look to position and title as a reason for respect, knowledge, and obedience, not the pastor's gifts, calling, or personal walk with Jesus. Questioning a pastor then is often seen as disrespectful, prideful, and rebellious. A sort of fear develops among leadership, resulting in vague answers to their pastor's questions, or giving a response they know the pastor wants to hear. Not that it matters anyway, because most of the time when seeking leadership input, many pastors have no intention of taking it seriously because he has already made up his mind. His asking is simply a kind gesture or formality.

The following all-too-common scenario is often the outcome; While on paper a church leadership group can seem like a caring and involved team, the reality is, everyone knows that their opinion doesn't matter because the pastor will make all the decisions anyway. It is not uncommon for those who disagree with the pastor to be seen as a threat and/or to be talked about behind their backs. Although on the outside most people would not know it, the lead pastor almost always protects the role as the main leader and decision-maker which leads to the above misfortunes.

Many North American churches do, however, appoint elders as part of their leadership structure. Although this is a positive and biblical attribute, unlike what we learn in the New Testament, NAC elders are typically expected to remain behind the scenes and are often unknown to the congregation. Interestingly and ironically, elders often tend to make most major church decisions such as hiring and firing staff, how to use church finances, and making other big decisions that affect the whole church. Even though most North American churches do appoint elders, their appointment is rarely consistent with Scripture. Appointed elders not only have biblically defined roles to play but also biblically defined qualifications that are often not met. Scripture defines not only the role of an elder but also the qualifications to be one:

The saying is trustworthy: If anyone aspires to the office of overseer, he desires a noble task. Therefore, an overseer must be above reproach, the husband of one wife, sober-minded, self-controlled, respectable, hospitable, able to teach, not a drunkard, not violent but gentle, not quarrelsome, not a lover of money. He must manage his own household well, with all dignity keeping his children submissive, for if someone does not know how to manage his own household, how will he care for God's church? - 1 Timothy 3:1-7*

This is why I left you in Crete, so that you might put what remained into order, and appoint elders in every town as I directed you— if anyone is above reproach, the husband of one wife, and his children are believers and not open to the charge of debauchery or insubordination. For an overseer, as

*God's steward, must be above reproach. He must not
be arrogant or quick-tempered or a drunkard or
violent or greedy for gain, but hospitable, a lover of
good, self-controlled, upright, holy, and disciplined.
He must hold firm to the trustworthy word as taught,
so that he may be able to give instruction in sound
doctrine and also to rebuke those who contradict it.* -
Titus 1:5-9

*So I exhort the elders among you, as a fellow elder
and a witness of the sufferings of Christ, as well as a
partaker in the glory that is going to be revealed:
shepherd the flock of God that is among you,
exercising oversight, not under compulsion, but
willingly, as God would have you; not for shameful
gain, but eagerly; not domineering over those in your
charge, but being examples to the flock. And when
the chief Shepherd appears, you will receive the
unfading crown of glory.* - 1 Peter 5:1-4

This chapter has outlined outside influences and positional
power, agendas, and their impacts on churches in North
America. As we look forward, we must continue to assess the
church structure currently in place by revisiting the church
structure found in Scripture. The next chapter will walk us
through biblical elements that can help equip you for this
assessment.

19

Post-Chapter Assessment Questions

1. What elements might you need to change in your current church structure?

2. How do you think churches can change the "butts in seats" mentality? Why or why not?

Chapter 2

Pre-Chapter Assessment Questions

1. How would you define community?

2. Do you feel that your current church functions as a community? How or how not?

3. What of the five spiritual gifts given in Ephesians 4:16 are represented and used in your current church structure?

Community Minded

I think it is safe to say everyone longs for community. Whether communities are found surrounding local high schools, sports teams, video games, clothing styles, or the current rally around cryptocurrency like *Bitcoin* or *Dogecoin*, there is something special about being part of a community. This is, in part, what made the New Testament Church (NTC) so attractive. In the New Testament, the church was founded on and operated under a decentralized organizational structure. Decentralized does not mean unorganized, but rather it means that the church was not reliant on or seen as an institution or organization. Where the North American Church (NAC) functions more like a business, the NTC functioned as a community:

> *They devoted themselves to the apostles' teaching and to fellowship, to the breaking of bread and to prayer. Everyone was filled with awe at the many wonders and signs performed by the apostles. All the believers were together and had everything in common. They sold property and possessions to give to anyone who had need. Every day they continued to meet together in the temple courts. They broke bread in their homes and ate together with glad and sincere hearts, praising God and enjoying the favor of all the people. And the Lord added to their number daily those who were being saved.* – Acts 2:42-47

...so that there should be no division in the body, but that its parts should have equal concern for each other. If one part suffers, every part suffers with it; if one part is honored, every part rejoices with it. Now you are the body of Christ, and each one of you is a part of it. - 1 Corinthians 12:25-27

And let us consider how we may spur one another on toward love and good deeds, not giving up meeting together, as some are in the habit of doing, but encouraging one another and all the more as you see the Day approaching.
- Hebrews 10:24-25.

This community function was a major defining characteristic of the church in the New Testament. What and who made up this community? If according to the Merriam-Webster Dictionary, a *community* is "a unified body of individuals" and is, in the present context, "a group of people who have the same interests, religion, race, etc." Furthermore, we agree that the Bible teaches us that the church functioned as a community, and the biblical term for *church* in all cases is *ecclēsia (or some form of it meaning the same thing)*. Thus, the only conclusion is that *the church* and *a church* are made up of believers, followers of Jesus. There is no other option.

Uniqueness Matters

It is important to realize that each community is unique and different communities will have different outward reflections of the biblical church. For example, a church in rural Tennessee will look dramatically different than a church in urban Chicago. Although this is often the case, the different outward reflections must not contradict the Bible's teachings about the church. In trying to explain this, Will Mancini uses the unique signature of snowflakes as an example of the uniqueness found in individual communities in his book *Church Unique*. He compares God's plan for churches with snowflakes in that no two snowflakes are the same. The point here is that each church should be unique because each community is unique. Yet, as the foundational elements of all snowflakes are found in the scientific elements of water, the foundational elements for a church are found in scripture.

Individual church communities will be made up of people with unique needs, gifts, and desires. Here are a few examples found in Scripture:

For by the grace given me I say to every one of you:
Do not think of yourself more highly than you ought,
but rather think of yourself with sober judgment, in
accordance with the faith God has distributed to each
of you. For just as each of us has one body with many
members, and these members do not all have the

same function, so in Christ we, though many, form one body, and each member belongs to all the others. We have different gifts, according to the grace given to each of us. If your gift is prophesying, then prophesy in accordance with your faith; if it is serving, then serve; if it is teaching, then teach; if it is to encourage, then give encouragement; if it is giving, then give generously; if it is to lead, do it diligently; if it is to show mercy, do it cheerfully. -
Romans 12:3-8

Now to each one the manifestation of the Spirit is given for the common good. To one there is given through the Spirit a message of wisdom, to another a message of knowledge by means of the same Spirit, to another faith by the same Spirit, to another gifts of healing by that one Spirit, to another miraculous powers, to another prophecy, to another distinguishing between spirits, to another speaking in different kinds of tongues, and to still another the interpretation of tongues. All these are the work of one and the same Spirit, and he distributes them to each one, just as he determines. - 1 Corinthians 12:7-11, 27-31

So Christ himself gave the apostles, the prophets, the evangelists, the pastors and teachers...
- Ephesians 4:11

This transpires through the NTC in Corinth, Galatia, and Ephesus. Although there are clear instructions in the Bible on how the church should be structured, this does not mean uniqueness justifies straying from the biblical foundational structural elements.

26

So Christ himself gave the apostles, the prophets, the evangelists, the pastors and teachers, to equip his people for works of service, so that the body of Christ may be built up until we all reach unity in the faith and in the knowledge of the Son of God and become mature, attaining to the whole measure of the fullness of Christ. -Ephesians 4:11-13

What then shall we say, brothers and sisters? When you come together, each of you has a hymn, or a word of instruction, a revelation, a tongue or an interpretation. Everything must be done so that the church may be built up. If anyone speaks in a tongue, two—or at the most three—should speak, one at a time, and someone must interpret. If there is no interpreter, the speaker should keep quiet in the church and speak to himself and to God. Two or three prophets should speak, and the others should weigh carefully what is said. And if a revelation comes to someone who is sitting down, the first speaker should stop. For you can all prophesy in turn so that everyone may be instructed and encouraged. The spirits of prophets are subject to the control of prophets. For God is not a God of disorder but of peace—as in all the congregations of the Lord's people. Women should remain silent in the churches. They are not allowed to speak, but must be in submission, as the law says. If they want to inquire about something, they should ask their own husbands at home; for it is disgraceful for a woman to speak in the church. Or did the word of God originate with you? Or are you the only people it has reached? If anyone thinks they are a prophet or otherwise gifted by the Spirit, let them acknowledge that what I am writing to you is the Lord's command. But if anyone ignores this, they will themselves be ignored.

27

Therefore, my brothers and sisters, be eager to prophesy, and do not forbid speaking in tongues. But everything should be done in a fitting and orderly way. - 1 Corinthians 14:26-40

Here is a trustworthy saying: Whoever aspires to be an overseer desires a noble task. Now the overseer is to be above reproach, faithful to his wife, temperate, self-controlled, respectable, hospitable, able to teach, not given to drunkenness, not violent but gentle, not quarrelsome, not a lover of money. He must manage his own family well and see that his children obey him, and he must do so in a manner worthy of full a respect. (If anyone does not know how to manage his own family, how can he take care of God's church?) He must not be a recent convert, or he may become conceited and fall under the same judgment as the devil. He must also have a good reputation with outsiders, so that he will not fall into disgrace and into the devil's trap. In the same way, deacons are to be worthy of respect, sincere, not indulging in much wine, and not pursuing dishonest gain. They must keep hold of the deep truths of the faith with a clear conscience. They must first be tested; and then if there is nothing against them, let them serve as deacons. In the same way, the women are to be worthy of respect, not malicious talkers but temperate and trustworthy in everything. A deacon must be faithful to his wife and must manage his children and his household well. Those who have served well gain an excellent standing and great assurance in their faith in Christ Jesus.
Although I hope to come to you soon, I am writing you these instructions so that, if I am delayed, you will know how people ought to conduct themselves in God's household, which is the church of the living

God, the pillar and foundation of the truth. Beyond all question, the mystery from which true godliness springs is great:
He appeared in the flesh,
was vindicated by the Spirit,
was seen by angels,
was preached among the nations,
was believed on in the world,
was taken up in glory. - 1 Timothy 3:1-16

To the elders among you, I appeal as a fellow elder and a witness of Christ's sufferings who also will share in the glory to be revealed: Be shepherds of God's flock that is under your care, watching over them—not because you must, but because you are willing, as God wants you to be; not pursuing dishonest gain, but eager to serve; not lording it over those entrusted to you, but being examples to the flock. And when the Chief Shepherd appears, you will receive the crown of glory that will never fade away. In the same way, you who are younger, submit yourselves to your elders. All of you, clothe yourselves with humility toward one another, because "God opposes the proud but shows favor to the humble."
- 1 Peter 5:1-5

Each church was uniquely designed based on the community they served according to God's designed expectations. The Bible also shows us in 1 Corinthians 9:19-23 that Paul understood this well and adjusted his lifestyle to better minister to people based on the uniqueness of each community:

29

"Though I am free and belong to no one, I have made myself a slave to everyone, to win as many as possible. To the Jews I became like a Jew, to win the Jews. To those under the law I became like one under the law (though I myself am not under the law), so as to win those under the law. To those not having the law I became like one not having the law. To the weak I became weak, to win the weak. I have become all things to all people so that by all possible means I might save some. I do all this for the sake of the gospel, that I may share in its blessings. –
1 Corinthians 9:19-23

Can It Really Be That Simple?

A few years back, while living in Puerto Rico, I recall having a conversation with a fellow missionary and friend. I was explaining to him what the church was from a biblical perspective. I will never forget the silence that followed and his comment, which broke it. The simplicity of it was the problem. He grew up in a traditional North American church, and the simplicity which I was explaining was hard for him to grasp. This is a common response I get.

Although personal realities may differ, the simplicity is clear when looking at the church from a biblical perspective. The church functioned in public spaces or homes and would adjust to the life patterns of the local church members:

Every day they continued to meet together in the temple courts. They broke bread in their homes and ate together with glad and sincere hearts...
- Acts 2:46

30

You know that I have not hesitated to preach anything that would be helpful to you but have taught you publicly and from house to house. - Acts 20:20

Greet also the church that meets at their house. - Romans 16:5

The churches in the province of Asia send you greetings. Aquila and Priscilla a greet you warmly in the Lord, and so does the church that meets at their house. - 1 Corinthians 16:19

Give my greetings to the brothers and sisters at Laodicea, and to Nympha and the church in her house. - Colossians 4:15

also to Apphia our sister and Archippus our fellow soldier—and to the church that meets in your home: - Philemon 1:2

A complicated church structure would have been seen as absurd to the historically biblical Christians.

Who Is The Greatest?

Who is the greatest? This is not a new question being asked by the church. It is as old as the New Testament Church. People have always wanted to know who is better, who is more qualified, and who is greater, and whoever this is, is often who people think should be in charge. In Luke, we read about an argument that transpired which sought answers to just these questions; *"An argument started among*

31

the disciples as to which of them would be the greatest" (Luke 9:46). Greatness equaled power, and power equaled being in charge. Jesus had, what I can imagine, was an unexpected response, *"Jesus, knowing their thoughts, took a little child and had him stand beside him. Then he said to them, "Whoever welcomes this little child in my name welcomes me, and whoever welcomes me welcomes the one who sent me. For it is the one who is least among you all who is the greatest"* (Luke 9:47-48). What a slam this had to be on the disciples' egos. Later in Scripture, we find out that Jesus never intended the church to be led by one person of power, but rather multiple people with different gifts

> *So Christ himself gave the apostles, the prophets, the evangelists, the pastors and teachers, to equip his people for works of service, so that the body of Christ may be built up until we all reach unity in the faith and in the knowledge of the Son of God and become mature, attaining to the whole measure of the fullness of Christ.* -Ephesians 4:11-16

Jesus saw the gifts as foundational and necessary for the church then and he still does today. If the church is ever going to grow in maturity these gifts must be utilized within the church. Jesus understood community well.

What About Chaos?

Chaos seems to have mostly negative connotations. But if you have ever been part of any community, you know very well that chaos (family issues, personal issues, community issues, etc.) is bound to take place and, at times necessary to grow as a community. Although no one individual should be placed in charge over the church, God does desire order amidst the chaos and has designed roles to help us fulfill his purpose for the church.

God's way of bringing order to the chaos is through the appointing of elders and we observe Paul in Titus 1:5 charging the disciples in Crete to do this; *"The reason I left you in Crete was that you might put in order what was left unfinished and appoint a elders in every town, as I directed you"* (see also Acts 14:23, 20:1720:28; 1 Timothy 3:1-16, 5:17; James 5:14; and 1 Peter 5:1-5). In contrast to many North American churches, pastoral ministry extends far beyond the leadership of the pastor. In the NTC, elders were the leaders of the church, not the pastor alone. In discussing the proper outline for church, Jim Tomberlin points to the New Testament Church, specifically the Antioch church. The idea of a team structured leadership team, according to Tomberlin, was exactly what the Antioch church in Acts 13 displays. It had a leadership team composed of a rag-tag group of which many Christians would frown upon today. Tomberlin describes for us the team members; a Jewish rabbi (Saul of Tarsus), a Jewish marketplace leader (Barnabas), a North African (Niger), a Jewish aristocrat (Manaen), and a cosmopolitan Roman (Lucius). This rag-tag team of believers represents the best example of a world-changing, life-giving, sending church in the Bible. Moreover, a biblical leadership model of a church consists of elders, not staffed positions.

No Position Available

"Sorry, there is no pastoral position available here. We do welcome your gift of pastoring though." Sadly, if this was a posting on a job board the likelihood of this church receiving applicants is slim. But this speaks to the unbiblical structure found within many North American churches does it not? A defining leadership element found in the church of the New Testament is that *all leaders* were *elders*, and *all elders* played an important role in the community life of the church. We find no distinction between pastor and elder in Scripture. To a degree, the two were synonymous with each other and there was no division among them:

> *For by the grace given me I say to every one of you:*
> *Do not think of yourself more highly than you ought,*
> *but rather think of yourself with sober judgment, in*
> *accordance with the faith God has distributed to each*
> *of you. For just as each of us has one body with many*
> *members, and these members do not all have the*

same function, so in Christ we, though many, form one body, and each member belongs to all the others. We have different gifts, according to the grace given to each of us. If your gift is prophesying, then prophesy in accordance with your faith; if it is serving, then serve; if it is teaching, then teach; if it is to encourage, then give encouragement; if it is giving, then give generously; if it is to lead, do it diligently; if it is to show mercy, do it cheerfully. Love must be sincere. Hate what is evil; cling to what is good. Be devoted to one another in love. Honor one another above yourselves. Never be lacking in zeal, but keep your spiritual fervor, serving the Lord. Be joyful in hope, patient in affliction, faithful in prayer. Share with the Lord's people who are in need. Practice hospitality.
- Romans 12:3-13

I appeal to you, brothers and sisters, in the name of our Lord Jesus Christ, that all of you agree with one another in what you say and that there be no divisions among you, but that you be perfectly united in mind and thought. - 1 Corinthians 1:10

...so that there should be no division in the body, but that its parts should have equal concern for each other. If one part suffers, every part suffers with it; if one part is honored, every part rejoices with it. Now you are the body of Christ, and each one of you is a part of it. - 1 Corinthians 12:25-27

Do nothing out of selfish ambition or vain conceit. Rather, in humility value others above yourselves, not looking to your own interests but each of you to the interests of the others. In your relationships with one another, have the same mindset as Christ Jesus:

35

*Who, being in very nature God, did not consider
equality with God something to be used to his own
advantage; rather, he made himself nothing by
taking the very nature of a servant, being made in
human likeness.
And being found in appearance as a man, he
humbled himself by becoming obedient to death -
even death on a cross! Therefore, God exalted him to
the highest place and gave him the name that is
above every name, that at the name of Jesus every
knee should bow, in heaven and on earth and under
the earth, and every tongue acknowledge that Jesus
Christ is Lord, to the glory of God the Father.
Therefore, my dear friends, as you have always
obeyed—not only in my presence, but now much more
in my absence—continue to work out your salvation
with fear and trembling, for it is God who works in
you to will and to act in order to fulfill his good
purpose. Do everything without grumbling or
arguing, so that you may become blameless and pure,
"children of God without fault in a warped and
crooked generation."
Then you will shine among them like stars in the sky
as you hold firmly to the word of life. And then I will
be able to boast on the day of Christ that I did not
run or labor in vain.* - Philippians 2:3-16

There is no indication in the New Testament of the pastor

being referred to as a *position* as understood today, it is only

referred to as a *gift*. Moving forward, it should be understood

that pastors (elders) were placed in churches to equip the

body to go out and do the work:

Then the eleven disciples went to Galilee, to the mountain where Jesus had told them to go. When they saw him, they worshiped him; but some doubted. Then Jesus came to them and said, "All authority in heaven and on earth has been given to me. Therefore go and make disciples of all nations, baptizing them in the name of the Father and of the Son and of the Holy Spirit, and teaching them to obey everything I have commanded you. And surely I am with you always, to the very end of the age." - Matthew 28:16-20

To the elders among you, I appeal as a fellow elder and a witness of Christ's sufferings who also will share in the glory to be revealed: Be shepherds of God's flock that is under your care, watching over them—not because you must, but because you are willing, as God wants you to be; not pursuing dishonest gain, but eager to serve; not lording it over those entrusted to you, but being examples to the flock. And when the Chief Shepherd appears, you will receive the crown of glory that will never fade away. In the same way, you who are younger, submit yourselves to your elders. All of you, clothe yourselves with humility toward one another, because, "God opposes the proud but shows favor to the humble." - 1 Peter 5:1-5

as well as care for the local church body. One further point I will make on the posting of pastoral positions, or any church position for that matter, is this; if a church needs to post a position opening, doesn't that reflect the lack of discipleship taking place within that church? If a local church is making disciples in a biblically sound manner, there will be no need to

37

post openings because the church will have been discipling others who are called and capable to fulfill those roles.

Post-Chapter Assessment Questions

1. Take some time to reflect on how your local church might better produce a biblical community of believers?

2. How would your church be different if leadership was structured like the New Testament Church?

3. Would most people consider your church structure simple or complicated? Why?

4. If simple, how can you teach this to others?

5. If complicated, what needs to change, and are you willing to do it?

Chapter 3

Pre-Chapter Assessment Questions

1. What is the main goal of your church?

2. How is the whole body reaching that goal?

3. How does your church expect people to hear about Jesus?

4. How does your church gage fruit?

5. How many times in the past decade has your church added new attraction-based elements (i.e., new worship styles, new programs, sanctuary ambiance, building remodel, etc.)?

Fruit Check

The institutional church is an amazing feat when you think about it. Somehow, leaders of the NAC have managed to convince people that the church is a location or building and, in that form, is an important aspect of the Christian faith. We hear it called "The House of God", "God's House", "The Temple of God", and so on. Yet, the Bible teaches us in 1 Corinthians 6:19 that we are God's temple; *"Do you not know that your bodies are temples of the Holy Spirit, who is in you, whom you have received from God?"* As a result of this false understanding, people give *millions of dollars* each year to building funds, projects, and other specified funds that are needed for "the church" to run. Not to mention the tithes and offerings that come in for paying staff, maintenance needs, supplies, debt, and other costs of operating the organization.

According to *Lewis Center for Church Leadership*, "Lovett Weems reminds us that visitors often form a first impression of a church based on the appearance of the areas they first encounter, such as the parking lot, entry, and restrooms. He recommends four steps to assess and improve the message sent to newcomers by the condition of your facilities." While these "needs" are being met with little question, a father who just lost his job needs to apply to a church program and take budget classes for help and a single mother who needs groceries for her three children must humiliate herself by going to a food pantry and/or applying for food stamps, then is looked down upon because of it.

Warren Bird's research reveals half of a church's budget goes to pay staff. For churches with worship attendances of 2,000 or more, the total debt average is 66% of the church's annual budget. This is insane. Iannaccone, Olson, and Stark discuss in their article *Religions and Church Growth, Social Forces* a similar mindset towards church growth by concluding,

> A religious organization cannot survive, much less grow, unless it obtains sufficient resources from the environment. Congregations need places to meet and people to lead them; church structures cost money to build and maintain; outreach, evangelism, and community service demands time and money; the activities of ministers, music directors, Sunday school teachers, and janitors never come free, even when supplied by volunteers.

Bird's, Iannaccone's, Olson's, and Stark's findings are representative of a consistent mindset towards church growth in North America. E.M. Bounds has been quoted saying, "Money has materialized the church. The money she does not give has earthened her. Money-loving, money-making, money-keeping is the rock on which the spiritual movements of the church are stranded." In essence, the NAC structure demands a continued stream of money to function, and this demand does not include any personal needs of church members or giving done by the church.

The article *Religions and Church Growth, Social Forces* further this thought,

> Growth can occur only if there are surplus resources, such as time and money beyond the minimum required to maintain current operations and to compensate for depreciation in physical facilities and in membership lost to death or departure.

All this is done under the guise, the bigger or better the church, the more people will come, hear, and give. If the idea of being bigger and better continues to be the focus of church growth, it may be possible that more people will walk through the front doors, sit in the seats, hear a message, and give to some degree. However, this is hardly the case for the church as a whole. Ferreira and Chipenyu find that church membership trends reveal a consistent decline within Protestant churches around the world. They continue to report, "Krejcir (2007:1) notes that American Protestant churches declined by 5 million members (i.e., 9.5%) from 1990 to 2000. He adds that half the churches did not add new members for two years preceding 2007." Even if local church numbers do increase, numbers rarely equate to people being reached with the truth, maturing in their faith, or being obedient to the truth, which is the purpose of a church.

According to the Bible, if the NAC structure was working for kingdom advancement the above-stated numbers would not only be significantly less but reversed from decreasing to increasing. The fact that the North American Church is on the decline should indicate that the structure is not biblical, thus whatever is accepted as working is not working to produce the right kind of fruit.

Special Effects

With an attraction-based, come and hear, church structure for the purpose of numerical growth, an often-unrecognized problem arises, or maybe it is less unrecognized as it is denied. The problem is *truth*, or the lack of it to be more precise. Truth historically has turned more people away than it has attracted. Jesus' message to the crowd about drinking His blood and eating His flesh, needing to be born again, and the cost of following him are just a few biblical examples. To be fair, this issue with truth extends much further than just the church. We have been conditioned to accept non-truths as truth in many facets of our lives. One example can be found in the use of special effects in movies.

Some of my favorite movies are about espionage. In a way I guess this makes sense because espionage is what was taking place when the Gospel began to spread, and when the church was founded. A man or woman meeting death at every corner in the attempt to retrieve or deliver information that could change the world, while their enemy is hot on their heels trying to stop them, often from the inside. Will they complete their mission? Will the world be saved? What unbelievable predicament will they find themselves in next? Will they get shot? Will they get thrown in prison, making a miraculous escape? We all know the ending, so what is it about movies that cause us to keep coming back? Two words: *Special Effects.*

Most of us know that a fender bender does not cause a car to explode, jumping from a three-story building will likely kill you, and a punch to the face does not make that cool thump-shoosh-thud sound, yet we rarely question the truth of any of this while watching our favorite movie. In fact, we enjoy it and continue to come back for more.

This may seem like a far leap from church structure, but it is important to understand why film producers use special effects as it correlates with the NAC structure. Maybe Ed Sikov's definition of special effects will help,

> The term special effects is broadly defined as any image or element within the image that has been produced by extraordinary technical means. ...in excess of the ordinary technology necessary for the production of motion pictures.

To paraphrase, special effects are elements used to produce something that is not naturally present to enhance what is naturally present.

Although many people enjoy special effects, they may not always enjoy what is obviously false. Münsterberg describes the film experience as a *'unique inner experience'* that due to the simultaneous character of reality and pictorial representation "brings our mind into a peculiar complex state." This *'unique inner experience'* is what creates a fascination for movies and their apparent reality. People desire reality, even if that reality is created and fake, as long as the fake stimulates the senses in a pleasing manner. Many people, however, do not want the truth. The Bible reveals this in 2 Timothy 4:3, *"For the time will come when people will not put up with sound doctrine. Instead, to suit their own desires, they will gather around them a great number of teachers to say what their itching ears want to hear."* Thus, when the truth of God's Word creates friction in one's reality, the natural derivative is to seek the "truth" or "reality" that meets his or her personal satisfactory criteria. For a reason similar to film producers, a majority of NACs use their own type of special effects like art, videos, dramatic word, stage lights, fog, big bands, darkened sanctuaries, dynamic speakers, and aesthetic decor. Based on Münsterberg's description of special effects purpose, these special effects used by churches bring the minds of those attending service "*into a peculiar complex state*". Thus, special effects are used in churches throughout North America presenting a pleasing reality that often results in numerical growth and financial increase. Sadly, based on what has been defined as special effects, the result is compromised truth.

The church then, when operating under an institutional structure with a focus on attracting people with programs, building features, and entertainment must adjust the truth they share. Most leaders within NACs are not intentionally lying; however, many are leaving out certain truths, which is lying. Why would they do this? The answer is simple, *money*. Now, please hear me say this. I do not believe that the NAC and her leaders are money hungry, greedy, or have an intentional underlying motive of making money. The need to make money is a natural outcome of the NAC structure itself. Let me explain.

With more people comes the need for a bigger building, which comes with the need for more money, which further complicates the organizational structure. Weems believes, "A building is not an end in itself, but it can either help or hurt your mission of reaching and serving others in the name of Christ." This adds to the evidence that many NACs view the building as an integral part of the church. Sara Joy Proppe, for The Gospel Coalition, in the article titled *Come On In! 10 Tips for Welcoming Guests into Your Church Building*, suggests decorating the outside, marking a sidewalk, making the front door obvious, pleasing threshold transitions, using art or a bench as a marker for the front door, having something for people to do as they wait, and signage are all important factors when building a church. If your goal is to build a hotel what Weems and Proppe suggest should be seen as important factors. But if your goal is to grow the church as modeled for us by Jesus Christ these factors seem incompatible. Can you picture Jesus saying, 'Alright, I know this has been hard and a lot of people don't want to be part of the local church, and let me tell you why that is; you have not done a good job with the exterior-to-interior threshold transition, and the decorating is so drab where are all the paintings and nice toilet fixtures? And what are these people supposed to do while they wait for you to tell them about me, you don't expect them to talk to each other do you?' As ridiculous as this sounds, this is exactly the environment many NACs subconsciously teach and create. Again, I am addressing issues that are an outcome of the NAC structure itself, not NAC leaders.

One issue with the structural aspect of special effects within the NAC is that people are attracted to change. Every ten years or so, clothing styles change dramatically, housing styles change, desired vehicle types change, and so on. This often leads to forced change even if a person does not desire change. Clothing is a perfect example. We are limited in our clothing selection to what stores sell. Stores sell what the masses want (apparently people want men who wear a size 36 or larger to put on skinny stretch jeans because I cannot find a pair of regular denim non-stretch jeans to save my life). The NAC has done nothing different. Because attraction preferences change over time, worship styles change, the building features change, the ambiance changes, stage set-up changes, preaching styles change, and worst of all, what is accepted as truth changes. As a result, churches' financial needs grow, creating the need for higher church attendance. When the attendance need grows, the need to keep them coming grows. When the need to keep them coming grows, the need to keep them happy grows. When the need to keep them happy grows, the need to give them what they want grows. When the need to give them what they want grows, compromise is the result. There is no other option. *The structure demands the outcome.*

What was meant to be a community of Christians committed to and learning from one another, worshiping together, praying together, and meeting each other's needs (Acts 2:42-47), has turned into a not-for-profit business that depends on how many people come each week and how much money they give. This cannot be denied.

Before you get defensive, remember, typically this is an unintentional outcome that naturally derives from the structure itself which is based on a capitalist business model. Most NAC leaders have good intentions; however, the methods used to achieve them are inadequate and counterproductive resulting in a come-and-hear, consumer-driven church, rather than a grow-and-send, multiplication-driven church.

Post-Chapter Assessment Questions

1. What factors can you see within the local church that have resulted in an unintentional compromise of truth?

2. How can your church better minister the truth of the gospel?

3. Has money become a driving force in your church? If so, what needs to change?

Chapter 4

Pre-Chapter Assessment Questions

1. What does your church have in place to send people out into the world?

2. Does your church frequently ask the congregation to invite friends?

3. Are the church building and the Sunday gathering the primary focus of your church?

Community Life

What the North American Church (NAC) has accomplished is truly a feat. The New Testament Church (NTC) is a feat as well. However, not for the same reason. The church has lasted for more than 2,000 years and began not as meetings in large buildings, or as an organized ministry, but as followers of Jesus gathering in homes and communal meeting places up until roughly 330 A.D., during the reign of Constantine. Even though Constantine continued his pagan practices, he used Christianity and the church as a way to gain power and influence. It wasn't until the rule of Constantine that the original church structure began to deteriorate.

Constantine was willing to do whatever it took to gain power. When pagan practices did not work, he turned to Christian practices and the church. Money and power were clear motivators in Constantine's establishing of the church, not God's glory. What is seen in the book of Acts as a community of believers, functioning as the church to spread the gospel, we see turned into a mode of power, control, and profit. Sound familiar?

In the sense of everyday common life, how the NTC was lived out was not revolutionary. I was able to witness this firsthand, sort of. While my wife and I were on a trip to Israel, with Liberty University in 2019, we visited Magdala. If you are not aware (I was not), Magdala is the city where Mary Magdalen lived. I must admit, my wife and I were not thrilled about this stop, neither of us had ever heard of Magdala. Everything changed once we arrived. Magdala turned out to be one of the most powerful and impactful visits of our trip. What stood out to me the most was the amazing amount of structural details (foundations, streets, animal stales, etc.) preserved in there. I could picture people walking the streets and patronizing local businesses. I was truly left in awe. Life in Magdala was communal; there was one blacksmith, one leatherworker, one woodworker, etc., each utilized by the community as needed and the synagogue was the main focal point and a communal gathering spot. We were, literally, walking through what is described in Acts 2:42-46. The major difference found in communities like Magdala, where the church was present, was the why behind the what. This visit opened my eyes to what it means to be a true Christian community (see figure 2). Rather than for personal gain, Christian communities functioned to bring God glory and to spread the gospel (Acts 2:42-46). This was revolutionary, in the sense that the love Christians expressed towards each other and the sacrifices they made for each other were categorically unique, and are even still today.

Take a moment to read Matthew 5:21-48:

"You have heard that it was said to the people long ago, 'You shall not murder, and anyone who murders will be subject to judgment.' But I tell you that anyone who is angry with a brother or sister will be subject to judgment. Again, anyone who says to a brother or sister, 'Raca,' is answerable to the court. And anyone who says, 'You fool!' will be in danger of the fire of hell.

"Therefore, if you are offering your gift at the altar and there remember that your brother or sister has something against you, leave your gift there in front of the altar. First go and be reconciled to them; then come and offer your gift.

"Settle matters quickly with your adversary who is taking you to court. Do it while you are still together on the way, or your adversary may hand you over to the judge, and the judge may hand you over to the officer, and you may be thrown into prison. Truly I tell you, you will not get out until you have paid the last penny.

"You have heard that it was said, 'You shall not commit adultery.' But I tell you that anyone who looks at a woman lustfully has already committed adultery with her in his heart. If your right eye causes you to stumble, gouge it out and throw it away. It is better for you to lose one part of your body than for your whole body to be thrown into hell. And if your right hand causes you to stumble, cut it off and throw it away. It is better for you to lose one part of your body than for your whole body to go into hell.

"It has been said, 'Anyone who divorces his wife must give her a certificate of divorce.' But I tell you that anyone who divorces his wife, except for sexual immorality, makes her the victim of adultery, and

anyone who marries a divorced woman commits adultery.

"Again, you have heard that it was said to the people long ago, 'Do not break your oath, but fulfill to the Lord the vows you have made.' But I tell you, do not swear an oath at all: either by heaven, for it is God's throne; or by the earth, for it is his footstool; or by Jerusalem, for it is the city of the Great King. And do not swear by your head, for you cannot make even one hair white or black. All you need to say is simply 'Yes' or 'No'; anything beyond this comes from the evil one.

"You have heard that it was said, 'Eye for eye, and tooth for tooth.' But I tell you, do not resist an evil person. If anyone slaps you on the right cheek, turn to them the other cheek also. And if anyone wants to sue you and take your shirt, hand over your coat as well. If anyone forces you to go one mile, go with them two miles. Give to the one who asks you, and do not turn away from the one who wants to borrow from you.

"You have heard that it was said, 'Love your neighbor and hate your enemy.' But I tell you, love your enemies and pray for those who persecute you, that you may be children of your Father in heaven. He causes his sun to rise on the evil and the good, and sends rain on the righteous and the unrighteous. If you love those who love you, what reward will you get? Are not even the tax collectors doing that? And if you greet only your own people, what are you doing more than others? Do not even pagans do that? Be perfect, therefore, as your heavenly Father is perfect.

Today, at any given moment, we can hear church leaders talking about being a community. At first glance, this sounds wonderful. However, taking a closer look, the people within the community being referred to are those within the organization that has been labeled church. As Christians, our community is much broader and extends beyond any organization. Yes, the church/a church is a community of believers, however, we are to look at our social and local communities as well. When asked who our neighbor is, Jesus responded with what is recorded in Luke 10:30-37:

> *In reply Jesus said: "A man was going down from Jerusalem to Jericho, when he was attacked by robbers. They stripped him of his clothes, beat him and went away, leaving him half dead. A priest happened to be going down the same road, and when he saw the man, he passed by on the other side. So too, a Levite, when he came to the place and saw him, passed by on the other side. But a Samaritan, as he traveled, came where the man was; and when he saw him, he took pity on him. He went to him and bandaged his wounds, pouring on oil and wine. Then he put the man on his own donkey, brought him to an inn and took care of him. The next day he took out two denarii e and gave them to the innkeeper. 'Look after him,' he said, 'and when I return, I will reimburse you for any extra expense you may have.' "Which of these three do you think was a neighbor to the man who fell into the hands of robbers?" The expert in the law replied, "The one who had mercy on him." Jesus told him, "Go and do likewise."*

Jesus taught us that our neighbors are all people. Roland Muller reminds us in *The Messenger The Message The Community*, that for Christians, our community is not only our church family or where we live, but also where we work, play, and send our kids to gain an education. This was not a new concept in the New Testament. The NTC understood that the church was not a building, location, or institution, but the living, breathing, body of Christ, lived out in the lives of those who followed Him, *"or just as each of us has one body with many members, and these members do not all have the same function, so in Christ we, though many, form one body, and each member belongs to all the others"* (Romans 12:4-5; see also Ephesians 3:6, 4:16, 5:23-30; 1 Corinthians 12:12-31; Colossians 1:18, 3:14-16). The church essentially infiltrated every part of society, which is part of the reason it was so effective.

Post-Chapter Assessment Questions

1. How can your church better become a true Christian community?

2. How might your church better love each other, and those around you?

Chapter 5

Pre-Chapter Assessment Questions

1. Take some time to chart the leadership structure of your church.

2. Who makes most of the major decisions for your church (senior pastor, elders, associate pastor, board, church members...)?

3. How much does the input of church members play a role in these decisions?

Ideas and Decisions

The church, as a body, has many moving parts and each part plays a unique role. Because each body part (local follower of Jesus) will inevitably come up with different ideas, each thinking their idea is best, therefore, God's idea, getting all the parts to come to a unified decision is a difficult task. Recognizing this, the North American Church's leadership structure places *education, staff,* and *positional status* as the main foundational components used in the effort to guide the body parts. We will see later on that this is reflective of the capitalist idea of business success.

Personal experience has revealed that there is no shortage of ideas within any given church body. However, there does seem to be a shortage of understanding as to how to proceed with them in unity. One fundamental issue experienced is that people can tend to think that all good or helpful ideas come from God. Although at first, this may not seem to be an issue, what happens when ten people in a room, with ten different ideas, think this way? We must realize when presented with different ideas, that just because an idea is good or helpful does not mean it is from God, or from God for the current situation/context, necessarily. One simple, hypothetical, example is this:

A church needed a secretary. Leadership was seeking someone who understood the role and was good with

67

administrative duties. They put out an ad and interviewed several people. The search came to an end when there were two candidates left. Jackie was on fire for Jesus, was gifted in administration, and felt called to serve the local church but only had a few months of experience working in an administration role. Becky had several years' experience, had a mediocre relationship with Jesus, and did not feel called to necessarily serve in the local church, but needed a job. The church decided to hire the candidate with several years of experience because of the large budget, congregation size, and workload expected. A good, helpful, and practical idea, but probably not a God idea.

When presented with choices, such as which school to send our children to, where to live, what job to take, or who we spend time with, my wife and I often remind each other that *not all good ideas are God ideas*, and it is no different with the church/a church.

Back to the NAC's answer to this dilemma, a leadership structure with education, staff, and positional status as foundational components. Aubrey Malphurs, in *Advanced Strategic Planning: A 21st-Century Model for Church and Ministry Leaders,* points this out by describing what is eerily similar between a Fortune 500 company and the NAC's leadership. In almost any given church found in North America, you will find a governing board, pastor, staff, and any matriarch or patriarch as part of its core empowered leadership team. Because of this, if an idea is going to be acted upon, those in the above positions *must* support it. This hierarchy system of positional leadership excludes its body members as a whole, relying on positional power alone to make decisions.

Although this may result in a fine-running organization, university, or business, the implications of this type of leadership structure within the church are far-reaching. Malphurs continues,

> In most smaller churches, the board runs things, due to their high pastoral turnover...In larger churches... the staff often runs the church, and the board's role may involve monitoring the senior pastor or it may be a diminished role. In the smaller board-run churches, if the board does not support strategic thinking and acting, it will not happen.

Change within the NAC then relies solely on the leadership's acceptance of it, right or wrong.

This hierarchy system results in multiple problems for the expansion of the gospel, and the freedom in which Christians should walk as well. Through the placing of one person as the head, as the above structure indicates, the majority of church members will typically have very little, if any, say in decisions made for the church; *this includes decisions that affect the whole body*. It should be no surprise then, that ideas for the implementation of new strategies within a church that are presented by the general body are often rejected, if considered at all, by the pastor. There can be multiple reasons for this, and Malphurs suggests a couple of possibilities: The pastor's lack of awareness or understanding of the process, or resistance to change. Not only does this tell the church members that they are less important than the pastor, but it also takes away the responsibility of the body by putting it all on the pastor or positioned leaders. This type of structure results in a church that is led by *staff*, paid or unpaid. However, this is not the most damaging result. An even more concerning result is that the church body ends up relying on *staff* to fulfill the *commands of Christ* rather than fulfilling the *commands of Christ* themselves.

Leadership Flow

The leadership flow (Plan America) of a typical North American Church goes as follows (also see Figure 3):

The People Expect the Pastor to:
- Be trained
- Get more training
- Attend conferences
- Spend his time
- Teach
- Make decisions
- Be responsible for scheduling events
- Be responsible for creating programs
- Be responsible for developing a worship experience
- Be responsible for handling unforeseen issues (both in and out of the church body)
- Minister to the sick
- Make visits

The resulting outcome is the pastor is also responsible for:
- Evangelism
- Discipleship
- Teaching
- Preaching
- Member care
- Fulfilling the Great Commission

This inevitably leads to limited family time for the pastor, ultimately causing ministry burnout. This often leads to the pastor's resignation (personally decided or forced). Harold Senkbeil points out, in *Church Leadership &*

71

Strategy: For the Care of Souls: For the Care of Souls,
that people are beginning to recognize the unhealthy
overemphasis on church leadership, coining the term,
"leadership emphasis fatigue." Lance Ford also is
concerned with leadership obsession in the church. It is
pointed out that Jesus himself contradicts a majority of
what the North American Church calls leadership today.
Furthermore, although people are leaving their homes to
serve Jesus in the mission field, the above leadership flow
does not allow for others to be equipped and sent out.
Watchman Nee, a 1930's Chinese missionary, addresses
yet another reality. Rather than being sent out by their
local church, many Christian workers have simply gone
out. This is tragic because not only do these workers go
out lacking support from their local church, but division is
also an all too often outcome; it is also contrary to what
Jesus prays in John 17, *"...so that they may be one as we
are one"* (John 17:11b). With this said, the hierarchical
leadership style of the NAC seems even more inadequate
for a church to be a church Jesus Christ desires and
designed. We will describe the leadership model found in the
NTC, in the next chapter, offering ways in which biblical
leadership principles and methods can be implemented in the North
American Church today.

Post-Chapter Assessment Questions

Looking at the chart you drafted at the beginning of this chapter...

1. What does your church need to change about its leadership structure?

2. How do you plan on doing this?

3. What can you change to take the load off of your pastor and leadership and better equip the whole body?

Awakening The Sleeping Giant

Chapter 6

Pre-Chapter Assessment Questions

1. Is your church allowing the whole body to use their gifts?

2. How does your church gauge maturity?

3. How does it plan on growing in maturity?

4. Do you view some roles as more important than others?

A Five-Fold Structure

The Bible details a church that relies on the entire body to fulfill its mission. When Jesus gave the five-fold gifts to the church (evangelist, prophet, apostle, pastor, and teacher) the expectation was that each local church body would include these five gifts:

For just as each of us has one body with many members, and these members do not all have the same function, so in Christ we, though many, form one body, and each member belongs to all the others. We have different gifts, according to the grace given to each of us. If your gift is prophesying, then prophesy in accordance with your a faith; if it is serving, then serve; if it is teaching, then teach; if it is to encourage, then give encouragement; if it is giving, then give generously; if it is to lead, b do it diligently; if it is to show mercy, do it cheerfully. - Romans 12:4-5*

So Christ himself gave the apostles, the prophets, the evangelists, the pastors and teachers,
- Ephesians 4:11

Without them Jesus says that a church cannot become a mature church:

And he gave the apostles, the prophets, the evangelists, the shepherds, and teachers, to equip the saints for the work of ministry, for building up the body of Christ, until we all attain to the unity of the faith and of the knowledge of the Son of God, to mature manhood, to the measure of the stature of the fullness of Christ. - Ephesians 4:11-13, ESV

77

Nee knew this was an issue and felt the need to address it already in the 1930s. He wrote,

> The first thing we must realize is that God has incorporated all His children into one body. He recognizes no division of His people...He has designed that all who are His shall live a corporate life, the life of a body among whose many members there is mutual consideration, mutual love, and mutual understanding.

When writing to his churches, Paul never saw himself as better than the others, nor more important. He wrote in Philippians 3:10-13:

> *I want to know Christ—yes, to know the power of his resurrection and participation in his sufferings, becoming like him in his death, and so, somehow, attaining to the resurrection from the dead. Not that I have already obtained all this, or have already arrived at my goal, but I press on to take hold of that for which Christ Jesus took hold of me. Brothers and sisters, I do not consider myself yet to have taken hold of it.*

To the church in Galatia he wrote, "*May I never boast except in the cross of our Lord Jesus Christ, through which the world has been crucified to me, and I to the world*" (Galatians 6:14). Paul, furthermore, understood his role as an apostle. He did not try to persuade those who had the gift of pastoring, for example, to do what he did because he knew their gifting was different, thus their work would be different (Acts 6:1-7).

North American Christians tend to look at the world through their, personal, spiritual gift glasses, thinking the rest of the church sees or should see things just as they do. It goes like this:

- The evangelists wonder why others spend so much time in Bible studies and church services when we could be out preaching the *Word of God* because people are dying and going to Hell.
- The pastors wonder why more people don't come to church on Sunday to hear the *Word of God* because if people don't come how will they know?
- The apostles wonder why people focus on sharing the *Word of God* in ever-growing large churches when we could be planting many smaller churches around the world because multiplication works better than addition.
- The teachers wonder why more people don't take studying the *Word of God* seriously and want to teach everybody everything because people won't know if they are not taught.
- The prophets see the *Word of God* in everything and wonder why no one else sees it because the world is spiritual.

What we need to do as Christians, is adjust our spiritual gift vision, understanding that each member plays a different and vital role, and this is exactly what we see in the New Testament Church.

It is no surprise that people are different. Therefore, it should be no surprise that God does not intend his church to be structured with one or two giftings/people. If the church is the body of Christ, which we believe to be the case, a local church must be made up of all the giftings given to the church by Jesus Christ.

For example, football runs through our family's DNA. Our oldest son, Blake, has played football since he was five years old. Over the years, as I watched Blake's teams beat other teams with significant physical advantages, I learned a lot about football. The main element of the game that stands out is the necessity of working as a team. His middle school team went undefeated, losing in the finals because of some unfortunate events outside of the team's control. The reason they made it that far was because they worked together. No one player was viewed more highly than the other. The same goes for his high school team, which won many games, making it to the playoffs every year. Again, there was no single position that was viewed more highly than the others. For every drive, each player had his own unique role to play, but when one player missed his play, the entire team was affected. The church body is no different. If the pastors and teachers are the only ones playing in the game, there is no possible way the church will be healthy, eventually losing the game. Without the other 'players' the church will remain dead and/or immature.

Paul understood this well and shared how the NTCs struggled with this from time to time, with details of how he corrected them. Some examples of how Paul corrected the different churches are; making appeals, asking questions, giving commands, and re-preaching the gospel (1 Corinthians, 2 Corinthians, Galatians). Although the church missed it often, a five-fold structure of leadership is evident in the New Testament. The Bible points to not only the church needing the five-fold leadership structure, but that it is a waste of time, energy, and giftings if church members are serving in areas outside of their gifting, or not serving at all. In the apostles addressing the issue of food distribution, it was said, *"It is not desirable that we should leave the word of God and serve tables"* (Acts 6:2). It is not that the apostles looked at waiting on tables as a lowly cause, or less important, rather it was, according to St. Pierre,

> Because their calling was to preach and witness to the lost, the apostles felt their focus should be on teaching the gospel, and advancing the truth about Jesus, the risen Christ rather than concentrate on benevolence and the distribution of food to the poor.

If the twelve would have waited on tables, they would have been wasting the gift and calling placed on them by Jesus. It would be like a defensive lineman being asked to play quarterback and the quarterback being asked to play on the defensive line.

When the whole body is equipped, the church grows in maturity. When only parts of the body are expected to do all the work, the fruit is limited, and maturity remains in a stalemate or worse, declines. Thus, the five-fold leadership structure found in the New Testament Church is the leadership structure which the church should be applying today.

Post-Chapter Assessment Questions

1. How has your local community suffered because of a lack of equipping the whole body?

2. What can your church do to better equip the whole body?

Chapter 7

Pre-Chapter Assessment Questions

1. How much emphasis does your church put on growing in numbers?

2. How important is formal education concerning your church leadership staff?

A Consumer Minded Church

As Christians living in North America, because of capitalism, we have been taught to be consumers our entire lives, often without even realizing it. From elementary school to doctorate programs, we have been taught that knowledge is power. The more you gain the more you have. The United States' third president, Thomas Jefferson, based his entire career on this philosophy, and a letter from Elisha Ticknor revealed how the teaching world accepted his philosophy as well. The North American Church is no different. The structure of the NAC is consumer-based, with a 'come and hear,' 'knowledge is power' mentality (see figure 4). In countless sermons, church members around the United States have heard, "Invite your friends next week", "If people are going to go to church that normally do not, Easter and Christmas are the days they will come. Invite your friends and family." Recently a pastor stated, "I will do whatever it takes to get people to come to church to hear the Word of God. We need to give them what they want so we can give them what they need". Another pastor has recently said, "Anything short of sin we are willing to risk to bring people closer to Jesus". Concerning how late-modern churches have connected with people, Don Corder writes in *Connect: How To Grow Your Church In 28-Days Guaranteed,* "Most of the connection

87

methods were passive and rear-loaded. They were passive in that they were dependent on the new visitor initiating the connection." He explains further, "The church would wait for the visitor to fill out the connection card, visit the connection center, register for a new member's class, attend Sunday school, or request a meeting with the pastor." Corder even has a chapter titled "Throw a Party" that describes what he calls "reach events" to *attract* non-believers to attend church. Corder shares ideas such as chili cook-offs, a carnival, a car show, showing Disney movies, inviting a food truck to the event, and making the event free for all as means to get non-believers to the church. The unintended outcome of these "reach events" is that it creates a consumer mindset, both in those coming and those who throw the party." According to online dictionary *Merriam-Webster,* the word "consumer" is a noun that is typically used as an attribute and means, "one that utilizes economic goods." The concept is contrary to what we find in the New Testament. In Jesus' Great Commission we find *"go and make..."*. When Jesus healed the demon-possessed man in Mark chapter 5, He said *"go and tell..."*. The only time Jesus ever used the word "come" was when calling people unto Himself, *"Let the little children come..."* (Matthew 19:14; Luke 18:16; Mark 10:14), *"Come to me all you weary..."* (Matthew 11:28), *"No one comes to the Father except through me..."* (John 14:6). Simply put, by looking at the definition of "consumer" as well as using biblical evidence of what the church should look like, the NAC has been acting contrary to the command, *"go and make"*, that Jesus gives his disciples Matthew 28:18-20.

One reason for this "come and hear" mentality in the NAC, which results in church members being consumers rather than producers, is that knowledge is understood not only to be powerful but also is considered the essential part of being a Christian. This is evident in church job requirements alone. In a Discipleship Pastor position for a local church, their knowledge requirement is listed in the job description,

> A Master's Degree from an approved seminary with 5+ years of experience is preferred.

And another church lists,

> Bachelor's and/or master's degree in biblical and theological studies. An emphasis in discipleship is preferable.

The NAC has taught, even if subconsciously, that Christians should not step into ministry until they have the appropriate knowledge, and they should not teach others or share with others until they have been obedient themselves. Which, creating a giant anti-productive circle, cannot be done unless they have enough knowledge. Look at how much churches spend annually on leadership conferences, church development conferences, or other knowledge/ new method-focused conferences alone. The cost for a conference can be between $99 a person and upwards of $1,000 a person, and this generally does not include lodging, food, or transportation. Outside the dollar amount spent, are annual conferences really worth it? After all, if what was taught at these annual conferences worked, would there be a need to go to more? Yet, churches continue to send their staff year after year.

The persistent problem is that there is never enough knowledge to be gained (Proverbs 1:5; Romans 11:33; Colossians 2:2-3; 2 Peter 3:18), and the amount of knowledge required is judged differently by different people. There is no quantitative, "common standard" for knowledge one is expected to gain. In his book *Do What Jesus Did*, Robby Dawkins reminds us that "God isn't necessarily looking for qualified people; He's looking for *available* people whom He can use." Dawkins' view of God is quite contrary to the NAC's insistence on gaining knowledge.

Post-Chapter Assessment Questions

1. What would your church need to change to become a producer-minded church rather than a consumer-minded church?

2. Who within your church might God want to use that you have overlooked because of a lack of formal education? How can you utilize them and their gift?

Chapter 8

Pre-Chapter Assessment Questions

1. What does your church hope to produce (churchgoers, met budget, bigger budget, saved people, larger staff, disciples, churches, etc.)?

2. How does it plan on producing those things?

3. Is your church producing disciples who make disciples?

New Testament Church Growth

The New Testament Church (NTC) was action-based.
Although knowledge was necessary, knowledge was not the
goal of the NTC, but rather action. Jesus expected the church
to go into the world (Matthew 10:7, 28:19-20, Mark 5:18-19;
16:15; Acts 1:8). When asked to define "disciple," Putman
quotes Matthew 4:19, *"Come, follow me," Jesus said, "and I
will send you out to fish for people."* Jesus, in calling his first
disciples, calls them to *follow* Him, and He will *send them
out*, making them fishers of men. Jesus was not asking these
men to follow Him into the synagogue; He was asking them to
literally follow Him by living like and doing as He did. Later,
this is confirmed in Matthew 28:20, *"teaching them to observe
all that I have commanded you."* Thus, it should be no
surprise, as Dawkins writes, that "The proclamation and
demonstration of the Kingdom of God was the central aspect
of Christ's ministry of reconciliation." If this was central to
Christ's ministry, as Dawkins claims, this is also an
expectation Christ has for the church today.

The pattern of New Testament church growth occurs in
three steps:

1. *Acts 2:41 - The gospel was preached* (in public spaces
   or private property).
2. *Acts 2:42-46 - There was a noticeably different lifestyle
   that followers of Jesus were living.*
3. *Acts 2:47 - God caused the increase.*

As the above biblical church growth pattern reveals, *Christians never expected to invite others to a church service. Jesus was all about going.*

Church growth in the New Testament was a natural outcome of Christians being obedient to Jesus after counting the cost of following Him (Matthew 4:18-22, 8:22, 19:21; Mark 8:34-36; Luke 9:57-62, 14:26-33). Jesus told Peter that *He* would build *His* church and that Peter was the rock on which *He* would build (Matthew 16:18). In contrast to the NAC, which attempts to promote growth by the local church's attractiveness (building, programs, great preachers, entertainment, worship style, etc.), Scripture clearly teaches us the cost of following Jesus comes with a price that begins with a personal choice and will to follow (put faith in/believe in) Him. Only after the cost was counted and accepted did the NTC founders disciple people. Those who were discipled were expected to act on the knowledge they received immediately:

> *As Jesus was getting into the boat, the man who had been demon-possessed begged to go with him. Jesus did not let him, but said, "Go home to your own people and tell them how much the Lord has done for you, and how he has had mercy on you." So the man went away and began to tell in the Decapolis how much Jesus had done for him. And all the people were amazed.* - Mark 5:18-20

> *He replied, "Blessed rather are those who hear the word of God and obey it." - Luke 11:28*

96

"If you love me, keep my commands. - John 14:15

Peter and the other apostles replied: "We must obey God rather than human beings! - Acts 5:29

Although the word "immediately" is not specifically used, it is implied when the Bible teaches us to act in obedience.

My wife has this saying that our kids have heard a hundred times, and it applies here too, "Delayed obedience is disobedience." James, Jesus' brother, makes the expectation of immediate obedience evident:

> *But be doers of the word, and not hearers only, deceiving yourselves. For if anyone is a hearer of the word and not a doer, he is like a man who looks intently at his natural face in a mirror. For he looks at himself and goes away and at once forgets what he was like. But the one who looks into the perfect law, the law of liberty, and perseveres, being no hearer who forgets but a doer who acts, he will be blessed in his doing.*
> - James 1:22-25 ESV

The Result of Obedient Christ Followers

As a result of the NTC's immediate response to the commands of Christ, the gospel was spread, the church grew, and the world was changed forever.

This biblical model significantly contrasts the centralized institution with big budgets, staff, buildings, and an underlying but necessary motive of getting butts in the seats found in almost every traditional church in North America.

The expectation Jesus places on his disciples to immediately apply what is learned empowers us to *go* minister the gospel, regardless of our biblical intellect or relational depth. This expectation also reveals the need for a five-fold leadership structure. For a church functioning under the biblical model, the church leadership flow will be as follows:

The leadership flow (Plan Bible) of a New Testament Church (NTC) model goes as follows (also see Figure 3):

The Elders Expect the People to:

> ➢ Get trained
> ➢ Train others
> ➢ Attend conferences
> ➢ Teach
> ➢ Help make decisions
> ➢ Build community through relationships

The resulting outcome is the **WHOLE CHURCH** is also responsible for:

> ➢ Evangelism
> ➢ Making Disciples
> ➢ Teaching
> ➢ Preaching
> ➢ Member care
> ➢ Fulfilling the Great Commission

This inevitably leads to more family time, disciples who make disciples, the lost being reached, and healthy multiplying churches being developed.

Rather than relying on the pastor to fulfill a majority of leadership roles, each church member was expected to use their spiritual gifts to minister in their own unique way. The resulting outcome was and still is revolutionary. Consisting of obedient followers of Jesus and leadership made up of elders, churches were decentralized communities of believers, intentionally bringing Jesus to the lost, hurting, and broken through their everyday lives.

Post-Chapter Assessment Questions

1. What could it look like if your church stopped inviting non-believers to the church service and expected the church to reach them outside of the local church gathering by intentionally living their lives to minister the gospel?

2. How many people do you know personally (not hearsay or a third party) within your church who *regularly* share the gospel, lead people to faith in Christ, and baptize people (other than staff).

3. What can your church do to decentralize and become a church known for followers of Jesus living every day to reflect Him and reach people for Him through their own life of faith?

Chapter 9

Pre-Chapter Assessment Questions

1. So far, what are the structural elements that have been highlighted for change within your church?

The Gathering

It should be of no surprise that the North American
Church (NAC) places the Sunday morning gathering as the
climatical highlight of church events, especially Easter and
Christmas. So much so that the largest portions of primary
church resources, such as *time, effort, and money,* are
budgeted for their preparation and facilitation. Brant
Henshaw's research reveals budgeting for payroll is by far the
NAC's largest expense. Henshaw reports that nearly half, or
47% of a church's budget is earmarked to pay salaries; seven
percent is used for property expenses, and ten percent is used
for program costs. Henshaw concludes that 64% or just under
two-thirds of a church's budget is primarily used for Sunday
morning service. These findings reveal the Sunday gathering
is the NAC's primary focus. However, this is not the case
found with the NTC.

The gathering in the NTC naturally developed as
disciples multiplied. Acts 2:42-47 prioritizes church unity and
spreading the Gospel over the actual gathering. Jesus
founded the church; its original function outlined in Acts is
the model all Christians are called to use. Furthermore, Acts
2:42-47 is the first mention of how the church operated and
includes its key elements. When the church gathered, it was a
result and natural outcome of believers' relationship with God

and each other. Today, many churches call the Sunday morning service "fellowship," however, according to Osborne, the fellowship referred to in Acts is more than just getting together. The Greek word used for fellowship is *koinonia,* which indicates contribution, participation, and sharing. The reason for the limited information about church gatherings in the New Testament is that it was not seen as the key aspect of the church. The *koinonia* found in Acts was representative of the whole life of the church, not just religious meetings. Thus, it is important to understand how the New Testament defines *the church* and *a church.*

The church is made up of all followers of Jesus. This is the universal church or body of Christ. Those who make up *the church* are individually and corporately meant to live out their lives reflecting Jesus Christ. As they gather as *the church,* they also gather as *a church. A church* is the local body of believers, the local expression of *the church:*

> *For where two or three gather in my name, there am I with them.* - Matthew 18:20

> *They devoted themselves to the apostles' teaching and to fellowship, to the breaking of bread and to prayer. Everyone was filled with awe at the many wonders and signs performed by the apostles. All the believers were together and had everything in common. They sold property and possessions to give to anyone who had need. Every day they continued to meet together in the temple courts. They broke bread*

*in their homes and ate together with glad and sincere
hearts, praising God and enjoying the favor of all the
people. And the Lord added to their number daily
those who were being saved.* - Acts 2:1, 2:42-47

*So when you are assembled and I am with you in
spirit, and the power of our Lord Jesus is present,*
- 1 Corinthians 5:4

*In the following directives I have no praise for you,
for your meetings do more harm than good. In the
first place, I hear that when you come together as a
church, there are divisions among you, and to some
extent I believe it. No doubt there have to be
differences among you to show which of you have
God's approval. So then, when you come together, it
is not the Lord's Supper you eat, for when you are
eating, some of you go ahead with your own private
suppers. As a result, one person remains hungry and
another gets drunk. Don't you have homes to eat and
drink in? Or do you despise the church of God by
humiliating those who have nothing? What shall I
say to you? Shall I praise you? Certainly not in this
matter!
For I received from the Lord what I also passed on to
you: The Lord Jesus, on the night he was betrayed,
took bread, and when he had given thanks, he broke
it and said, "This is my body, which is for you; do this
in remembrance of me." In the same way, after
supper he took the cup, saying, "This cup is the new
covenant in my blood; do this, whenever you drink it,
in remembrance of me." For whenever you eat this
bread and drink this cup, you proclaim the Lord's
death until he comes.
So then, whoever eats the bread or drinks the cup of
the Lord in an unworthy manner will be guilty of*

105

*sinning against the body and blood of the Lord.
Everyone ought to examine themselves before they
eat of the bread and drink from the cup. For those
who eat and drink without discerning the body of
Christ eat and drink judgment on themselves. That is
why many among you are weak and sick, and a
number of you have fallen asleep. But if we were
more discerning with regard to ourselves, we would
not come under such judgment. Nevertheless, when
we are judged in this way by the Lord, we are being
disciplined so that we will not be finally condemned
with the world.
So then, my brothers and sisters, when you gather to
eat, you should all eat together. Anyone who is
hungry should eat something at home, so that when
you meet together it may not result in judgment.
And when I come I will give further directions.*
-1 Corinthians 11:17-34

*What then shall we say, brothers and sisters? When
you come together, each of you has a hymn, or a word
of instruction, a revelation, a tongue or an
interpretation. Everything must be done so that the
church may be built up. If anyone speaks in a tongue,
two—or at the most three—should speak, one at a
time, and someone must interpret. If there is no
interpreter, the speaker should keep quiet in the
church and speak to himself and to God.
Two or three prophets should speak, and the others
should weigh carefully what is said.
And if a revelation comes to someone who is sitting
down, the first speaker should stop. For you can all
prophesy in turn so that everyone may be instructed
and encouraged. The spirits of prophets are subject to
the control of prophets. For God is not a God of*

disorder but of peace—as in all the congregations of the Lord's people.
Women should remain silent in the churches. They are not allowed to speak, but must be in submission, as the law says. If they want to inquire about something, they should ask their own husbands at home; for it is disgraceful for a woman to speak in the church.
Or did the word of God originate with you? Or are you the only people it has reached? If anyone thinks they are a prophet or otherwise gifted by the Spirit, let them acknowledge that what I am writing to you is the Lord's command. But if anyone ignores this, they will themselves be ignored.
Therefore, my brothers and sisters, be eager to prophesy, and do not forbid speaking in tongues. But everything should be done in a fitting and orderly way. - 1 Corinthians 14:26-40

And let us consider how we may spur one another on toward love and good deeds, not giving up meeting together, as some are in the habit of doing, but encouraging one another—and all the more as you see the Day approaching. - Hebrews 10:24-25

Church, as described in the Bible, is the ἐκκλησία (*ecclēsia),* and ἐκκλησία is the only word used for *church* in the Bible. According to the *Strong's Concordance,* ἐκκλησία are, "people called out from the world and to God, the outcome being the church (the mystical body of Christ) – i.e., the universal (total) body of believers whom God calls out from the world and into His eternal kingdom." The word, ἐκκλησία, is used in the Bible when referring to *a church* (an assembly or congregation), as well as *the church* (the whole body of Christian believers). With this understanding, we can now point to what the NAC must change concerning the gathering.

A recent trend in planting new churches is to start big. *ARC,* a church planting organization, suggests this on their church planting webpage in an article by Kevin Daughtry titled: *Who Really Cares About Your Church Launch?* Daughtry presents two points regarding launching big; "Start with raising awareness", and "Launch big with a concept built around a felt need." Although this method may work on an attractive and/or exciting level, resulting in large numerical church launches, the church is called not to use proven methods that "work", but rather, the church is called to use *proven biblical methods.* Just because something works, does not mean it is of the Lord. Hirsch and Catchim agree,

> ...if we take our Lord and the scriptures themselves at face value, then we already have everything we need to get the job done. The ecclesia is perfectly designed to achieve its distinctive mission, but to do so means that we must build according to code. We must work with Jesus in the power of the Holy Spirit to be the church that makes the difference that only we were designed to make. Only this idea of inherent design can explain why dynamic apostolic movements in history can have massive impact and growth with apparently very few of the resources we in the West think we need to get the job done. We are designed for world transformation; impact is built into the idea of ecclesia itself.

If these methods that man has created work, imagine what would happen if the church did what God has already given us!

Rather than starting with the goal of a large gathering of believers and growing in numbers, like most churches do today, starting small and multiplying is what we see in Scripture. Jesus did this when he called the first twelve disciples in Matthew 10 when he sent out the seventy-two in Luke 10:1-24, and this is also how the local church started in Acts 2:42-47. The 3,000 added to their numbers in Acts 2:41 were those added to *the church*. There is no indication that these 3,000 people ever gathered at one time in one location *on a regular basis*. The multiple mentions of churches that met in homes also point to a small gathering rather than a large one.

> *Day after day, in the temple courts and from house to house, they never stopped teaching and proclaiming the good news that Jesus is the Messiah.*
> - Acts 5:42

> *You know that I have not hesitated to preach anything that would be helpful to you but have taught you publicly and from house to house.* - Acts 20:20

> *Greet also the church that meets at their house.*
> - Romans 16:5

*The churches in the province of Asia send you
greetings. Aquila and Priscilla a greet you warmly in
the Lord, and so does the church that meets at their
house.* - 1 Corinthians 16:19

*Give my greetings to the brothers and sisters at
Laodicea, and to Nympha and the church in her
house.* - Colossians 4:15

*also to Apphia our sister and Archippus our fellow
soldier—and to the church that meets in your home.*
- Philemon 1:2

At the few large gathering's consisting of 3,000 to 5,000
people, *a megachurch by today's standards,* Jesus preached
the message, *"I am the living bread that came down from
heaven. Whoever eats this bread will live forever. This bread
is my flesh, which I will give for the life of the world."* (John
6:51), *"Jesus said to them, "Very truly I tell you, unless you
eat the flesh of the Son of Man and drink his blood, you have
no life in you. Whoever eats my flesh and drinks my blood has
eternal life, and I will raise them up at the last day"* (John
6:53-54), of which he never explained to those present mind
you, resulting in most of the people turning away; *"From this
time many of his disciples turned back and no longer followed
him"* (John 6:66). Scripture also reveals that Jesus performed
miracles, had the people leave, then left (Matthew 15:29-39),
performed a miracle, and immediately left (Mark 6:30-46).

Jesus was not interested in numbers; he was interested in *committed followers.* Consider the implications of Jesus' response to a question His disciples asked him. *"When he was alone, the Twelve and the others around him asked him about the parables. He told them,*

> *The secret of the kingdom of God has been given to you. But to those on the outside everything is said in parables so that, "'they may be ever seeing but never perceiving, and ever hearing but never understanding; otherwise they might turn and be forgiven!*
> - Mark 4:10-12

That is a major foundational problem with the NAC today; it seeks numbers, not committed followers of Jesus. *Again, please remember this is a natural byproduct of the NAC structure itself, not the church members, per se. The structure itself demands it.*

The Bible models simple, small gatherings or one-on-one encounters as the ministry setting for *reaching non-believers, making disciples, and growing relationships with one another.* Why would we use the large church gathering to invite non-believers, make disciples, or grow relationships if this is true? Specifically looking at inviting non-believers to a Sunday Service, this makes no sense. Why would we invite people to something they are not part of? Although God will use the

Sunday service to lead people to Jesus, that is not his desire. The Bible teaches us that God will even use what the devil meant for evil to bring him glory (Genesis 50:20; Romans 8:28), so we cannot use, "But look at what God has/is done/doing," as a justification for doing anything. Put yourself in the shoes of the non-believer you invite to church on Sunday, say an Atheist with strong Atheistic beliefs who has never had an encounter with Christianity to any positive extent, and what you are expecting them to do. You are asking them to (1) worship God, whom they don't believe in, (2) pray to God, whom they don't believe in, and (3) give money to the church, which they don't understand nor are they part of. Therefore, including discipleship and growing relationships again discipleship, relationship growth, and local church development should begin small, *just as modeled for us by Jesus and the first disciples.*

Furthermore, although non-believers can stay if they come in (1 Corinthians 14:23-25), the purpose of church gatherings is for local believers and is meant to encourage and equip them to *go out and make disciples.* Thus, reaching non-believers will be a natural outcome of any church gathering, big or small, leading to the multiplication of the simple gathering. Thus, the invitation of non-believers to a Sunday church *(ecclēsia)* service will not be necessary if *the church* is obedient to the commands of Christ. As the simple gatherings multiply, the church can come together as a regional church, although not as regularly as the simpler gathering. The regional church will include the five-fold gifts if healthy, simple gatherings are multiplying. There should be freedom of gift function to some degree; there is biblical evidence of order (1 Corinthians 14:1- 40). In other words, one example is if there are ten prophets in a regional gathering, not all ten have the freedom to speak freely.

As the regional church produces simple gatherings that spread outside the region, multiple regional gatherings will naturally develop. On an even less consistent basis, a whole-body gathering can take place. This gathering is made up of all regional churches within a given area. The purpose of these gatherings should be a celebration of what God is doing through the simple and regional gathering (Matthew 18:20; Hebrews 10:24-25; 1 Corinthians 14:26; 1 Thessalonians 5:11; Colossians 3:16). Again, the New Testament teaches that the gathering is not the goal. *The goal is reflecting Jesus, loving one another, and making disciples* (Matthew 28:19-20, 5:48; Mark 12:28-34; John 13:34-35, 15:12; Romans 12:2, 12:10, 13:8; 2 Corinthians 3:18; Colossians 3:10; Ephesians 4:24; 2 Corinthians 5:17; 1 Peter 4:8; 1 John 2:6, 3:18, 4:7-11, 4:20). *The NAC needs to shift its focus from the gathering to*

113

reflecting and loving Jesus, loving others, and making disciples, not just having the saying on their church sign. If the NAC were to follow these commands of Christ, there would be no need to plant churches as they would develop on their own. The church gathering will be the natural outcome of loving Jesus, loving others, and making disciples.

Church Ministries

The NAC's ministries and programs it relies on to attract people must also be reconsidered. There is little, if any, evidence of different ministries or programs being developed in the NTC. The only thing that seemed to attract people to the church was the gospel (Acts 2:37-41), and even the Gospel often turned people away. Everything else was a result of the believer's faith and obedience to the commands of Christ, not a new ministry. If the NAC followed the biblical church structure, there would be no need for attraction-based strategies. Attendees would already be part of the church body because the church would be reaching the lost, leading them to Jesus before Sunday even came around.

With that being said, what many NAC ministries do is important. However, rather than relying on the church as an organization to develop them, by being obedient to the Lord in the things already prepared for them, individual followers of Jesus can develop these ministries without the need of the church organization, *"For we are God's handiwork, created in Christ Jesus to do good works, which God prepared in advance for us to do"* (Ephesians 2:10). If the Lord lays on someone's heart a need to start ministering to youth, for example, they should do so. Ministries within the whole-body church (gathering of regional churches) can stem from simple church gatherings or regional church gatherings outside of any "official" church meeting and be led by lay leaders in the church:

> *In those days when the number of disciples was increasing, the Hellenistic Jews among them complained against the Hebraic Jews because their widows were being overlooked in the daily distribution of food. So the Twelve gathered all the disciples together and said, "It would not be right for us to neglect the ministry of the word of God in order to wait on tables. Brothers and sisters, choose seven men from among you who are known to be full of the Spirit and wisdom. We will turn this responsibility over to them and will give our attention to prayer and the ministry of the word."*
> *This proposal pleased the whole group. They chose Stephen, a man full of faith and of the Holy Spirit; also Philip, Procorus, Nicanor, Timon, Parmenas, and Nicolas from Antioch, a convert to Judaism. They presented these men to the apostles, who prayed and laid their hands on them.*
> *So the word of God spread. The number of disciples in Jerusalem increased rapidly, and a large number of priests became obedient to the faith.* - Acts 6:1-7

You, however, must teach what is appropriate to sound doctrine. Teach the older men to be temperate, worthy of respect, self-controlled, and sound in faith, in love and in endurance.

Likewise, teach the older women to be reverent in the way they live, not to be slanderers or addicted to much wine, but to teach what is good. Then they can urge the younger women to love their husbands and children, to be self-controlled and pure, to be busy at home, to be kind, and to be subject to their husbands, so that no one will malign the word of God.

Similarly, encourage the young men to be self-controlled. In everything set them an example by doing what is good. In your teaching show integrity, seriousness and soundness of speech that cannot be condemned, so that those who oppose you may be ashamed because they have nothing bad to say about us.

Teach slaves to be subject to their masters in everything, to try to please them, not to talk back to them, and not to steal from them, but to show that they can be fully trusted, so that in every way they will make the teaching about God our Savior attractive.

For the grace of God has appeared that offers salvation to all people. It teaches us to say "No" to ungodliness and worldly passions, and to live self-controlled, upright and godly lives in this present age, while we wait for the blessed hope—the appearing of the glory of our great God and Savior, Jesus Christ, who gave himself for us to redeem us from all wickedness and to purify for himself a people that are his very own, eager to do what is good.

These, then, are the things you should teach. Encourage and rebuke with all authority. Do not let anyone despise you. - Titus 2:1-15

The whole-body church would support these ministries, but they should not rely on the whole-body church to function (Acts 2:44-45; 1 Corinthians 16:1-4; 2 Corinthians 8:1-15, 9:1-15; 1 Timothy 5:17-18). By individual members of any church gathering launching and leading new ministries that meet either in homes or other neutral locations, the church will more efficiently and effectively fulfill the Great Commission. The more the body relies on a building or organization, the less likely it will make disciples.

The Building

One major aspect of the NAC that needs to change is the building. With multiple simple gatherings taking place in homes, regional gatherings taking place on a less frequent basis, and whole-body gatherings taking place quarterly, the need for a permanent building is not necessary. Instead, meetings can take place at a member's home/property, park, or outdoor public space. The church's freedom when there is no building tying them down to one location is part of the freedom we see Christians modeling in the New Testament.

Leadership

Leadership is the most critical change the NAC must make. Everything addressed in this book stems from the leadership style found in most NACs. This will likely be the most challenging hurdle for many to jump over.

117

As previously stated, the NTC was founded on a five-fold leadership consisting of evangelists, apostles, prophets, preachers, and teachers (Acts 1:8, 2:4, 19:6; 1 Corinthians; 12:7-11; Ephesians 4:11-16). Each gift given to the church must be used according to their gifting (Romans 12:6-8). I will address the role of a pastor in more depth because this is the gifting most associated with a position in traditional church settings. The role of the pastor can include regular teaching and preaching, but these are not to be the pastor's primary role. It is regularly debated if pastor and teacher were meant to be one gift or if the pastor was always the teacher. However, there is no reason to assume pastor and teacher are the same gifts other than possible grammatical evidence. There are plenty of pastors who struggle with teaching and teachers who struggle with pastoring. *Remember, we are referring to gifts, not functions or positions as traditionally viewed.* This does not mean that a pastor cannot teach, evangelize, start a ministry, or hear from God prophetically; it means that the Holy Spirit does not empower them to serve in those areas in the same way He does with those who have been gifted to do so. Thus again, the need for the five-fold ministry. Some examples of how the five-fold gifts can be used are on the next page.

Pastor
- Focus on caring for the whole-body church
- One-on-one discipleship
- Teaching/Preaching/Special teachings
- Pastoral Care needs

Teacher
- Teach at all gatherings as needed
- Teach scripture, not a "lesson" or "series"
- Teach how to apply scripture practically

Evangelist
- Regularly evangelizing/holding evangelistic meetings
- Teach evangelism to the church (teachings, modeling, assisting)
- Create evangelism outlets for the simple, regional, and whole-body church

Prophet
- Speak into gatherings concerning prophetic word
- Used as a buffer for less mature prophets
- Teach about prophecy and what it means today to the simple, regional, and whole-body church

Apostle
- Begin new works (simple church or individual ministries)
- Teach the church how to begin new works
- Help begin new regional church gatherings and whole-body gatherings

119

This is of course not an all-inclusive list, but I hope it helps paint a clear picture of the roles the five-fold plays in a church.

Through the multifaceted leadership found in the five-fold ministry, the workload is not only spread out, but the church will be more effective in fulfilling the mission at hand than if left to the pastor, as found in most NACs. Barry VanWyk, adamantly debates, "The five offices mentioned in Ephesians 4:11 are defined as roles and are considered necessary if a church wants to be a missional church as intended by Jesus Christ." The NAC often overlooks these gifts given by Jesus Christ to the church, and that must change. As a result of this change, the church will grow in maturity. The New Testament teaches that if *the church* operates *a church* under the biblical expectations, there will be no need to look at numbers because *God will bring the increase.*

By now, I hope you recognize that a much-needed change needs to take place in the North American Church. It will take time, and the work will be difficult. However, once the NAC understands that the institutional church and hierarchy leadership structure is contrary to what we find in the Bible and begins to apply the principles found in the NTC, the church will be unstoppable. We must trust God and his design for the church, even if it goes against everything our flesh thinks or feels is right. Often God does not make rational sense to our human minds because His ways are higher than ours. The church was meant to be a relational body of believers whose every aspect of life reflects Jesus. The NAC has turned what was meant to be relational into an institution that reflects a business more than it reflects Jesus. It is time for believers to stand up and fight for the church, the Bride of Christ. We must not let the world define who we are and what we do. We are the church; we are the sons and daughters of the one, true King Jesus; we are in the world, but not of it. Many may reject this research. Many may come against it with evidence, arguments, justifications, and alike, which is expected. Jesus tells us the path is narrow, and few will find it (Matthew 7:13-14). In other words, *the masses are typically wrong.*

In closing, I plead to those who completed this book, please, don't take my word for it. Whether you agree with the contents of this book or disagree, seek out the truth for yourself. Dig deep into God's Word, seek the Holy Spirit, and beg him to reveal the truth to you. I promise you; He will speak. This is not just another thing, another ministry, another option we are talking about. It is the Bride of Christ; the church, and she is too important to push off to the side.

Together we can awaken the Sleeping Giant. Wake up; now is the time. Jesus is coming back soon.

Post-Chapter Assessment Questions

1. Are you prepared to change?

2. What has God been speaking to you?

3. How do you plan on applying it?

Resource Index

Aronie, J. (2016). Do one thing every day that scares you. *The Federal Lawyer*. 17. https://www.sheppardmullin.com/media/article/1556_Aron ie%20IntheLegalComm.pdf

Bible Hub. (2021). Strong's Concordance. 1577. Ekklēsia. *Bible Hub*. https://biblehub.com/greek/1577.htm

Seabaugh, C. (Jul 23, 2020). The History of the Dodge Charger: A look back through the years at Dodge's venerable muscle car. *MotorTrend*. https://www.motortrend.com/features-collections/dodge-charger-history/

Batterson, M. (2012). Draw the circle. Zondervan Publishing.

Bird, W. (2013)."The economic outlook of very large churches", *Leadership Network*. PDF. 5.

Richards, Mary, et al (Directors). (2001). *Band of brothers* [TV series]. HBO Home Entertainment.

Hartwig, R. T. & Bird, W. (2015). *Teams That Thrive: Five Disciplines of Collaborative Church Leadership*. InterVarsity Press, 2015.

Mancini, W. (2008). *Church Unique: How Missional Leaders Cast Vision, Capture Culture, and Create Movement*. Jossey-Bass. 6.

Senkbeil, H. L. & Woodford, L. V. (2019). *Church Leadership & Strategy: For the Care of Souls: For the Care of Souls*. Lexham Press.

Merriam-Webster. (2021). *Merriam-Webster.com dictionary*. Retrieved on September 19, 2021, https://www.merriam-webster.com/dictionary/community

Weems, Jr., L. H. (2020, February 19). *4 Steps to a More Welcoming Church Building*. Lewis Center for Church Leadership. https://www.churchleadership.com/leading-ideas/4-steps-to-a-more-welcoming-church-building

Bird, W. (2013). The economic outlook of very large churches. *Leadership Network*. PDF.11, 13.

Iannaccone, L. R., Olson, D. V. A. & Stark, R. (December 1995). *Religions Resources and Church Growth, Social Forces.* 74 (2). 706. https://doi.org/10.1093/sf/74.2.705

Ferreira, I. W. & Chipenyu, W. (2021), Church decline: A comparative investigation assessing more than numbers, *In Die Skriflig,* 55(1), 1-10. https://dx.doi.org/10.4102/ids.v55i1.2645

Sikov, E. (2020). Eleven special effects, film studies, (2nd ed.). *Columbia University Press.* 2020. 158-168. https://doi.org/10.7312/siko19592-013.

Tan, E. S. (2018). A Psychology of the Film. *Palgrave Commun,* 4 (82) (2018). https://doi.org/10.1057/s41599-018-0111-y.

Münsterberg, H. (2001). *Hugo Munsterberg on Film: The Photoplay: a Psychological Study and Other Writings.* Taylor & Francis Group.

Weems, Jr., L. H. (2020, February 19). *4 Steps to a More Welcoming Church Building.* Lewis Center for Church Leadership. https://www.churchleadership.com/leading-ideas/4-steps-to-a-more-welcoming-church-building

Proppe, S. J. (2019, November 6). *Come On In! Tips for Welcoming Guests into Your Church Building.* The Gospel Coalition. https://www.thegospelcoalition.org/article/come-10-tips-welcoming-church-building

Mills, C. R. (2020). *The Consequences of the Christian Conversion of Constantine: Favoritism, Conflict, and Heresy.* https://history.hanover.edu/hhr/20/HHR2020-mills-constantine.pdf

Muller, R. (2013). *The Messenger The Message The Community: Three Critical Issues For the Cross-Cultural Church Planter,* (3rd ed.). CanBooks. 207.

Malphurs, A. (2013). *Advanced Strategic Planning: A 21st-Century Model for Church and Ministry Leaders.* Baker Books. 55, 56.

Senkbeil, H. L. & Woodford, L.V. (2019). *Church Leadership & Strategy: For the Care of Souls: For the Care of Souls.* Lexham Press.

Nee, W. (1994). *The Normal Christian Church Life.* Living Stream Ministry. 1994. 21, 25. (original work published 1957)

St. Pierre, D. (2012, November 11). *Acts 6:1-7 Seven Disciples Chosen to Manage Food Distribution to the Poor.* Thrive Through Christ. http://thrivethroughchrist.com/acts-61-7-seven-disciples-chosen-to-manage-food-distribution-to-the-poor

Bartlett, J. comp. (2000). *Familiar Quotations,* (10th ed.). rev. and enl. by Nathan Haskell Dole. Bartleby.com. www.bartleby.com/100

Founders Online. (1818, February 28). National Archives. *Elisha Ticknor to Thomas Jefferson.* https://founders.archives.gov/documents/Jefferson/03-12-02-0413. [Original source: The Papers of Thomas Jefferson, Retirement Series, vol. 12, 1 September 1817 to 21 April 1818, ed. J. Jefferson Looney. Princeton: Princeton University Press, 2014, pp. 512–514.]

Corder, D. (2019). *Connect: How To Grow Your Church In 28-Days Guaranteed.* HigherLife Publishing.18, 69.

Merriam-Webster. (2021). *Merriam-Webster.com dictionary.* Retrieved on September 19, 2021, https://www.merriam-webster.com/dictionary/community

Churchstaffing.com. (February 25, 2021). *Discipleship Pastor.* https://www.churchstaffing.com/job/247911/discipleship-pastor/brainerd-hills-baptist-church

Churchstaffing.com. (February 23, 2021). *Discipleship Pastor: Spiritual Formations and Connecting Generations.* https://www.churchstaffing.com/job/247847/discipleship-pastor-spiritual-formations-and-connecting-generations/first-baptist-church-boerne

Bento for business. (2020, January 8). *25 Non-Profit and Church Conferences for 2020.* https://bentoforbusiness.com/nonprofit/church-conferences/

Dawkins, R. (2013). *Do What Jesus Did.* Chosen. 77.

Putman, J., Harrington, B. W., Coleman, R. & Harrington, B. (2013). *Disciple Shift: Five Steps That Help Your Church to Make Disciples Who Make Disciples.* Zondervan Publishing. 45.

Henshaw, B. (2014, December 2). *How Churches Spend Their Money: 5 National Insights on Budget Priorities.* Pacific Northwest Conference of The United Methodist Church. https://www.pnwumc.org/news/how-churches-spend-their-money

Osborne, G. ed. (1999). *Life Application Bible Commentary: Acts.* Tyndale House Publishers. 38.

Wilkins, W. D., Lamberth, R. G., Fox, D. L., Harris, B. J., Hernández, E., Hukel, D. R., Pike Lambeth, R. S., Molina, S. P., Núñez, E. A., & Wetzler, D. L., eds. (1998). The Strongest NASB Exhaustive Concordance, NASB Update ed.: Zondervan. 1542. (original work published 1981)

Osborne, G. ed. (1999). *Life Application Bible Commentary: Acts.* 38.

Daughtry, K. (2020, July 9). *Who Truly Cares About Your Church Launch?* ARC. https://equip.arcchurches.com/who-truly-cares-about-your-church-launch

Barry, v. W. (2018). *The application of Ephesians 4:11 in the recent missional debate with reference to Scripture.* In Die Skriflig, 52(3). http://dx.doi.org.ezproxy.liberty.edu/10.4102/ids.v52i3.2305

Appendix

The following is not meant to be a set-in-stone organizational structure as that would defeat the whole purpose of writing this book. Instead, it is the best way I felt I could visibly lay out what the Bible teaches logically. Look beyond the 'structured layout' to the principles behind it.

What is Church?

The Church

The church is made up of all followers of Jesus. This is the universal church, the body of Christ. Those who make up *the* church are individually and corporately meant to live out their lives reflecting Jesus Christ. A church is the natural outcome of this.

A Church

A church is the gathering of believers that naturally develops due to the church's obedience to Christ.

- The local church: Made up of local believers who gather in a simple small group (homes, parks, or anywhere people gather).
- The regional church: Made up of regional believers from multiple local churches who gather in a simple larger group.
- The whole-body church: Made up of all believers in multiple reasons who gather in a simple much larger way.

The Church and *A* Church
Scripture Reference

- Matthew 18:20
- Acts 2:1, 2:42-47
- 1 Corinthians 5:4, 11:17-34, 14:26-40, Hebrews 10:24-25

Simple Local Church

- Gatherings of 10 people or less who meet frequently and regularly.
- This is where church multiplication begins.
- Simple local church gatherings are meant to focus on obedience to God, relationship building, discipleship, the study of God's Word, and accountability.
- Worship and prayer are essential aspects of the simple local church gatherings.
- Simple church gatherings are meant to be very basic in function following Acts 2:42-47.
- Local financial needs are met here. Giving comes from the heart, not a felt religious duty with a tithing mindset. Acts 2:44-45; 1 Corinthians 16:1-4; 2 Corinthians 8:1-15, 9:1-15
- A collection of funds, once local needs are met, can be taken up here and are to be used for needs within the local community. If no immediate need exists, regional elders can collect upon visiting. Corinthians 16:1-4

Regional Church

- The gathering of all simple local churches within a region who meet less frequently.
- Meant for corporate church worship, fellowship (eating, playing, etc.), prayer, testimonies, communion, and teaching.
- The five-fold ministry (apostle, prophet, evangelist, pastor, teacher) is to be represented here. Ephesians 4:11-16
- Giving doesn't occur in this setting as all giving takes place at each simple local church gathering. With the possible exception of a special need within the church body.

Whole-Body Church

- The gathering of multiple regional churches who gather as needed or desired, but significantly less frequently.
- This is for the corporate sharing of testimonies, fellowship, worship, prayer, preaching, and teaching.
- This is not to be used for inviting non-believers to "church." However, if non-believers come, they can join.
  1 Corinthians 5:5, 1 Corinthians 11:17-34, 12:13,27;14:24; Ephesians 1:22-23, 5:29-30.
  For the purpose of evangelism, a gospel presentation can be shared, and a call to faith made for the sake of the possible non-believers who come.
- Funds from the simple gatherings collected by regional elders are received by the whole-body elders and distributed to those in need, either within the body or the community (there should be no need for remaining funds). If funds remain, the elders can distribute as needed and or requested.

Acts 2:44-45; 1 Corinthians 16:1-4; 2 Corinthians 8:1-15, 9:1-15

- All needs within the whole-body church are to be met before meeting needs outside of the body. A healthy body will produce healthy work.
- Local church full-time and part-time workers come from the local body. There should be no need to look outside of the body for workers if the body is healthy.
- The focus is on church community, obedience to God's Word, and accountability.
- Individual gifts are expressed as the Spirit leads (should be tested).
- If the local church is healthy, those coming will already be involved in serving as the church in their simple local gatherings and regional church.
- All forms of ministry are the natural result of the church obeying Christ's commands. There is no need to develop programs or ministries if a church is a healthy biblically-based church.
- Teaching does not revolve around one person. Ephesians 4:11-16, Romans 12:6-8, 1 Peter 4:10-11
- The body members appoint Elders as the qualifications, gifts, and needs allow. Acts 6:1-15, Acts 14:23; 1 Timothy 5:17

Full-Time Sent Out Workers (Missionaries)

- Local full-time workers (those working primarily in ministry full-time in the general vicinity of the local whole-body church) are not considered sent-out workers. This does not mean the local body does not meet their financial needs. This is to be decided by each whole-body church. Local missionaries would likely receive less financial support than those sent out of the body.

- Full-Time sent-out workers are those who the Lord has called out of the local church body and the local church has sent out to reach areas outside the whole-body church area (typically a different country).
- Full-Time sent-out workers should be sent out via a calling from the Lord and with the financial support/sending of the whole-body church.
- Full-time sent-out workers cannot be new believers; for the sake of being prideful and lacking maturity.
- The whole-body church is responsible for fully financially supporting full-time workers they send out to the best of their ability.
- Full-time sent-out workers can be ordained as ministers of the gospel by the whole-body church. If the whole body supports the sending, the qualifications for ordination should already be met. No need to vet. Ordination represents the church's support of the sent out one, their faith, and fruit already being seen as a result of their life sold out for Jesus.

Church Ministries

All ministries within the whole-body church should stem from simple church gatherings or regional church gatherings outside of any "official" church meeting and be led by lay leaders. However, there could be a full-time or part-time dedicated pastor/elder to these people groups to aid in shepherding.

- Family/Children's gatherings
- Youth gatherings
- Men's gatherings
- Women's gatherings

(What is not meant by ministries is food ministries, homeless ministries, clothing ministries, etc. If the church is obeying the commands of Christ, there will be no need for these types of ministries as these are needs all Christians are called to meet with their individual lives as evidence of their faith.) James 2:14-26

Church Multiplication

- Simple local churches multiply by making disciples of Jesus who make more disciples of Jesus.
- Once a simple local church reaches its capacity, send out a small group to begin another simple local church.
- The regional church is made up of all simple local churches within a given region.
- The whole-body church is made up of all regional churches within any given nearby region.
- Suggested meeting locations
  o Simple local church: homes, parks, cafés, beaches, etc.
  o Regional church: larger spaces such as a barn, large home, public square, or other large public or semi-public areas.
  o Whole-body church: It may be necessary to rent a location for these gatherings (community hall, gymnasium, stadium, theater, etc.)
- Suggested meeting frequency:
  o Weekly: simple local church
  o Monthly: regional church
  o Quarterly or bi-annually: whole-body church

Elder Roles and Leadership Gift Roles

Elders

- Elders are to oversee local, regional, and whole-body churches.
- Elders' financial support should come from the church as needs present themselves and the church sees fit. 1 Timothy 5:17-18
- Elders are those who meet the biblical definition and qualifications of an elder and who the body appoints. Acts 6:1-7; Titus 1:5-9, 1 Tim. 3:1-7, 1 Peter 5:1-4
- Elders are like-minded and mature in their faith. Acts 6:1-7; 14:23
- Elders are whole-body appointed through prayer and seeking the Holy Spirits guidance: (*pastor, teacher, evangelist, prophet, apostle.*) Ephesians 4:1-16; 1 Timothy 3:1-13

Gift of Pastor

Care for and shepherd the local, regional, and whole-body church. Roles can include one-on-one discipleship, special teachings, and other pastoral care needs. This role can include regular teaching and preaching, but these should not be the main focus of pastors.

Gift of Teacher

Has the ability to teach at all gatherings as needed, one-on-one teaching/discipleship. Teachers also teach how to apply scripture practically.

Gift of Evangelist

Teaches evangelism to the body and one-on-one discipleship. The evangelist also intentionally creates evangelism outlets for the whole body.

Gift of Prophet

Has the ability to speak into situations in all gatherings. Mature prophets will disciple those who are less mature and test the spirit of other prophets. The prophet also teaches about prophecy and what it means today.

Gift of Apostle

Has the ability to teach church multiplication and help other body members begin their new work. The apostle also helps begin new regional church gatherings and whole-body gatherings as time and need allow.

137

Whole Body Leaders/Elders

- Regular contact with regional church bodies as well as simple local church bodies
- Teaching and Encouragement
- Collecting gifts from regional elders.
- Communication to the body through gatherings, visits, prayer times, etc.
- Responsible for distribution of funds based on known body needs
- Responsible for distribution of funds based on known community needs
- Held accountable by each other, regional elders, and the whole church body
- Hold regional elders accountable

Regional Leaders/Elders

- Same as whole body elders but only for their region
- Collecting gifts from Simple local church gatherings
- Held accountable by whole body elders and regional body members.

Appointed Pastors/Shepherds (included in elders)

- Shepherd the church
- Participate in simple local church gatherings by attending different ones
- Encouragement
- Communicate to simple local churches and regional churches
- Attend regional church gatherings
- Attend whole-body church gatherings
- Held accountable by all elders and church body members

- Other pastoral care needs as they arise (weddings, funerals, etc.)
- Teaches as the Spirit leads

Simple Gathering Facilitator

- Facilitate simple local church gatherings
- Host simple local church gatherings
- Collect funds from their simple local church gathering
- Hold simple local church members accountable
- Equip simple local church members to multiply more simple churches through discipleship
- Held accountable by regional elders and simple local church members

All Body Members

- Growing in faith and knowledge
- Growing in obedience to God's Word
- Growing in sharing what they are learning and obeying
- Meeting each other's needs
- Evangelism
- Discipleship (being discipled and discipling others)
- Be held accountable by simple church leaders and each other
- Being equipped for eldership/leadership

Church "Member" Accountability

- Regular accountability conversations with others
- Non-leadership role members are held accountable by their simple local church gathering facilitator
- Simple local church gathering facilitators are held accountable by a regional elder.

- Regional elders are held accountable by pastors, whole body elders, and church members.
- Pastors are held accountable by whole body elders, regional elders, and church members.

Figure 1: Church Gathering Flow

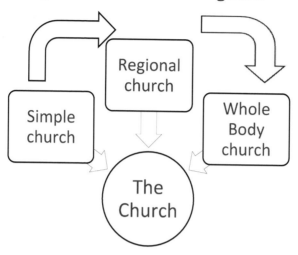

Figure 2: True Christian Community

Figure 3: Church Leadership Flow Plan-America

The People's Expectations

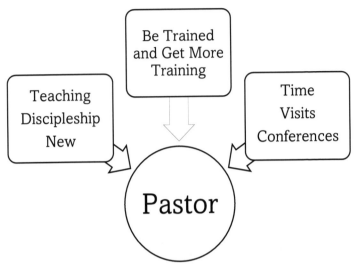

Church Leadership Flow Plan-Bible

Jesus' Expectations

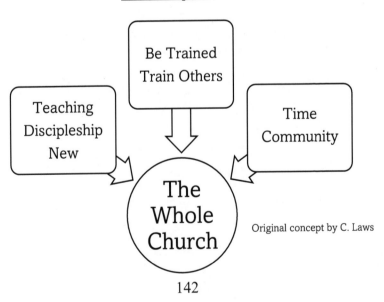

Original concept by C. Laws

Figure 4: Knowledge-Application-Sharing

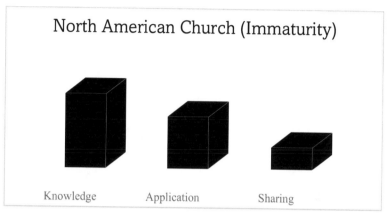

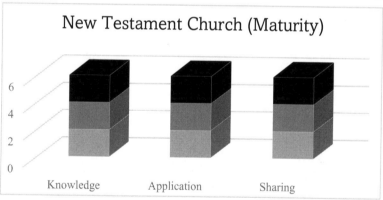

Original concept taken from: Making Disciples That Make Disciples
Module 1 – Full Version With Coaching Resources. www.big.life/training/training-module-1/

For more information on training

that can help in becoming

a more biblical model

of church, please contact us at:

www.bethechurch.training

It will be a blessing to

join you in your journey.